Turkish Embroidery

Turkish Embroidery

Gülseren Ramazanoğlu

VNR **VAN NOSTRAND REINHOLD COMPANY**
New York Cincinnati Toronto London Melbourne

Library of Congress Catalog Card Number 74-33892
ISBN 0-442-267991   (cloth)

All designs by Nuriye Gürkök Sabuncuoğlu unless otherwise credited.
All photographs by Sami Guner, unless otherwise credited.
Designed by Loudan Enterprises

Published in 1976 by Van Nostrand Reinhold Company
A Division of Litton Educational Publishing, Inc.
450 West 33rd Street
New York, NY 10001, U.S.A.
Van Nostrand Reinhold Limited
1410 Birchmount Road
Scarborough, Ontario M1P 2E7, Canada
Van Nostrand Reinhold Australia Pty. Ltd.
17 Queen Street
Mitcham, Victoria 3132, Australia
Van Nostrand Reinhold Company Ltd.
Molly Millars Lane
Wokingham, Berkshire, England

16   15   14   13   12   11   10   9   8   7   6   5   4   3   2   1

Library of Congress Cataloging in Publication Data

Ramazanoğlu, Gülseren.
    Turkish embroidery.

    1. Embroidery, Turkish.   I. Title.
TT769.T9R35   746.4'4   74-33892
ISBN 0-442-26799-1

Contents

Foreword and Acknowledgments

My interest in embroidery goes back to my childhood when we used to embroider simple table mats and napkins at school. Alas, my interest was short-lived. As the years went by I acquired many other interests that stole away my time from embroidery.

But to admire a beautiful embroidery or to appreciate a needlewoman with artistic talent does not require much time. So, I have become, ever since my school days, an appreciative observer. My interest in arts has led me to research for writing articles on various aspects of Turkish art, and it is a pleasant feeling to share the findings with those who are interested. It was an article of mine appearing in the Istanbul Hilton Magazine titled *Turkish Embroidery* that led to the opportunity for writing this book.

My first action was to consult Bedia Diker, the then director of Istanbul Olgunlashma Enstitüsü (Advanced Technical Institute for Girls in Istanbul) for help and guidance. She was kind enough to accept my request and let me use material from their

archives, photograph embroidered pieces, and visit the classes.

I cannot find words to express my gratitude to Nuriye Gürkök Sabuncuoğlu, one of the Institute's top-ranking teachers of technical drawing, with thirty years of experience. In spite of her exceptional talents she is modest and thoroughly enjoys teaching the art of drawing beautiful Turkish designs, a feeling I greatly appreciated when she enlightened me patiently in the field of embroidery. In addition to her creations from the archives of the Institute, she kindly let me use some designs which she keeps in her private archives. With the exception of a few dresses, everything in this book was designed by her. Since so much of the material in this book is taken from the archives of the Institute, created by Nuriye Gürkök Sabuncuoğlu, and embroidered in the Institute's *ateliers*, no more credit will be given in the captions of the pictures.

I would also like to thank Shükran Chinay, the new director of the Insti-

tute, who kindly let me continue my research and spend many pleasant hours in Mrs. Sabuncuoğlu's classes. Thanks also to Meral Ishik, one of her best students, who helped me in her spare time by marking the stitches on the line drawings.

I was given from the archives of the Institute designs pricked with a needle and thus ready to be transferred onto paper. For drawing the transferred designs I needed someone who could draw with patience and confidence. Aydin Erkmen, a leading Turkish graphic designer who illustrates the Istanbul Hilton Magazine which I edit, agreed to do this layman's job, in the time he could spare from his daily creative work.

I would like to thank Kemal Chiğ, curator of the Topkapi Palace Museum, who made it possible for me to visit the Turkish Embroideries Section before it was officially opened to the public and to photograph a royal *kaftan* from the sixteenth century. I also owe gratitude to Nurhayat Berker, chief of the Turkish Embroi-

Nuriye Gürkök Sabuncuoğlu

7

deries Section in the Museum, for explaining the valuable embroideries on display in her section and for briefing me on the history of Turkish embroidery.

One of Turkey's top photographers, Sami Güner, who specializes in photographing embroidery, took almost all the pictures in this book. Mr. Güner was quite happy at the prospect of presenting his exquisite photographs of Turkish embroideries to a wide public. Only the pictures taken by others will have photograph credits in the captions.

I owe a great deal to my family. My husband encouraged me to work when I had many other obligations. My eight-year-old son Can was quite understanding when I was studying rather than playing with him. He knew "homework" had to be done first. Most of my time was spent in research, collecting appropriate and informative documents and elegant designs to tempt my readers to embroider. I had no time to embroider myself, with the exception of few stitches to make sure that my descriptions were correct. I am still not even an amateur embroideress.

Nuriye Gürkök Sabuncuoğlu is a great professional in designing Turkish motifs, and you have in this book a large collection of her creations with which to begin your experiments in Turkish embroidery. I hope you benefit from the information I have gathered and her designs, and come to enjoy the beautiful colors, motifs, and stitches of Turkish embroidery.

Author and photographer

8

1 History of Turkish Embroidery

The art of embroidery has a long and fascinating history, dating back to pre-historic times. The earliest needles, made of fish or animal bones, metal or wire, have been found in many excavations, confirming man's persistent urge to decorate. Unfortunately, those early artists were not as adept in the preservation of cloth, and thus their work has been lost to us.

It is impossible to say where and when the art of Turkish embroidery actually had its birthplace. There are, however, some records indicating that, as in most other forms of art, this embroidery originated in Central Asia and travelled west with the nomadic Turks. The Uigur frescoes depicted soldiers with heavily embroidered uniforms; Seljuk miniature drawings were full of richly embroidered tents of the nomadic Turks. As they were always ready for war on horseback, they favored designs of stylized horses in their arts, but with the acceptance of the Moslem religion in the early part of the

ninth century, the animal motif gave way to floral designs.

In Moslem art, embroidery had a prominent place. It is intersting to note that the oldest known piece of embroidered cloth produced by the Moslems can be found in the Victoria and Albert Museum in London, with inscriptions suggesting a seventh or eighth century Kufic origin. The Lyon Museum in France treasures gold-embroidered pieces of cloth bearing the name of the famous twelfth-century Seljuk Turkish Sultan Alaeddin Keykubat.

Most of the ancient civilizations in Anatolia—from the Hittites, the oldest civilization, to the Byzantines and the Ottoman Turks—wore embroidered costumes and accessories. It is a common belief that wherever textiles existed, embroidered work was also to be found, however primitive it might have been. And Hittite textile samples dating to 6000 B.C. have been found in Alacahöyük, Turkey, thus giving indication of an extremely early origin.

Although there is no written record, it is a common belief that thousands of craftswomen worked inside or outside the palace to embroider garments, household items, and accessories only for the court. In the palace, embroidery was applied to every kind of cloth used for daily needs, including all varieties of men's wear.

As for the ladies' clothing, unfortunately there is not a single dress left extant from the court, but we know that dresses, as well as such items as underwear, shoes, scarves, handkerchiefs, veils, belts, gloves, tablecloths, curtains, prayer rugs, towels, and bridal gowns were all elegantly embroidered.

Palace embroidery influenced the common people to the extent that it became a folk art, and the embroideries eventually produced in the city of Istanbul were as exquisite as those produced in the palace. And, as individual artists embroidered with feeling, expression, and personal style, there are no two identical pieces of embroidered work.

Brides of the day took pride in embroidering their own trousseaux, and the custom of displaying a trousseau before the wedding provided an exchange of ideas for different designs, colors, and styles among the young girls. This tradition still continues in many Anatolian villages, and for this reason embroidery lives on in Anatolia today, having attained the level of a fine art.

Other than palace and home embroideries, there was a slightly inferior type produced by craftsmen in the market. It was also handmade but done to produce as much embroidery material as possible. For example, if the court embroiderers counted two threads for a stitch, the market embroiderers might count four. These mass-produced embroiderers were sold at less expensive prices.

The motifs used in the embroidery vary from village to village. As with the carpet motifs, every area retains its traditional designs. Similarly, because the art of embroidery is an inherited one, the technique, the color combinations, the designs, the secrets of root dyes, of weaving, and of silk-making, pass from one generation to the other, changing very little through the centuries. However, every period has its own distinctive color and motif preferences.

SIXTEENTH- AND SEVENTEENTH-CENTURY EMBROIDERIES

Although Turkish embroidery in Anatolia dates back to the early eleventh century, the techniques of fabric preservation were not as developed as the art itself, and examples of this early work have thus been lost to us.

In fact, the oldest examples of Turkish embroidery in existence today date from the sixteenth century (see color picture c-1), when some of the loyal servants of the Sultans began a new tradition of storing away the Sultan's garments and accessories as souvenirs. Although they had no access to modern-day chemicals to preserve the silk and the embroidery, other means were devised. The Turkish custom of placing personal clothing in a wrapping of up to forty *bohchas* (coverings) provided ample protection from deterioration. These coverings were made of a piece of cloth of any size or material, depending on need, but usually about one yard square. The object was placed in the center of the *bohcha* and then overlapped by first one corner, then the opposite corner, and finally the remaining two corners. The end result looked like an envelope.

As in all forms of Turkish art, the development of embroidery reached its peak in the sixteenth century. Simple motifs were used in an isolated fashion to decorate centers and borders. Pomegranates, artichokes, roses, tulips, carnations, hyacinths, leaves, and even pine cones enriched with spiral lines were used naturalistically or in stylized forms. The most frequently used colors were gold, red, green, blue, and sometimes cream or yellow. These sixteenth-century motifs preserved a basic simplicity which earned them the reputation of classical excellence.

The flowering of the art of the sixteenth-century embroideries gradually began to fade as the seventeenth century ran its course. The Turkish embroidery began to change its form and style through use of an increasing number of colors and motifs.

The simple outlines of the embroideries disappeared with the introduction of complex motifs, which were composed of a mixture of flowers, fruits, and leaves. Contrasting colors and lighter and darker shades of one color on a single piece of embroidery were the characteristics of this age.

EIGHTEENTH- AND NINETEENTH-CENTURY EMBROIDERIES

In the eighteenth century, the art of Turkish embroidery declined even further, and by the nineteenth century, gaudy colors and confused motifs were greatly in evidence, an indication of diminishing artistic value.

Whirligig motifs, naturalistic plant and fruit motifs (see color pictures c-2 and c-4), every kind of floral design (see color pictures c-3 and c-5), landscapes, mosques, trees, and houses were all employed. Flowers were arranged along twisting branches, and, as in other forms of Turkish art in this century, the style was baroque.

The number of colors were excessive, with eight to ten shades sometimes being used on one piece. Gold and silver threads, beads, pearls, and other valuable stones were introduced. The embroideries with valuable stones can be seen in Istanbul, in the Topkapi Palace Museum's Treasury Section.

CONTEMPORARY REVIVAL OF TURKISH EMBROIDERY

The establishment of the Girls' Technical Schools some 110 years ago made it possible for the young girls of the country to learn the art of designing, cutting, sewing and embroidering dresses. The most gifted and talented girls to graduate from the technical schools go on to specialize in Institutes that provide higher edu-

1-1. Landscape embroidered in the eighteenth century. (Collection of Istanbul *Olgunlashma Enstitüsü.*)

cation in embroidery. The exquisite work done by these young girls has been recognized by the government, and Turkish state gifts for the heads of foreign states are often prepared in their ateliers.

The institutes employ not only the older embroidery techniques but also copy patterns from old *chevres*, which are embroidered pieces of cloth, used in the household and as accessories to garments since the sixteenth century. Sometimes old designs inspire new stylized patterns (see color pictures c-4 and c-5). Color picture c-6 shows the original *chevre* from which patterns were copied to embroider a state gift for President Eisenhower.

One does not necessarily have to copy from an old embroidery. Any form of the Turkish art can become a source of inspiration from which you may draw your own Turkish pattern for embroidery, as many Turkish girls and women have done over the years. With this kind of creativeness, the art of Turkish embroidery will continue to live in all its glowing splendor.

2 Before Starting Turkish Embroidery

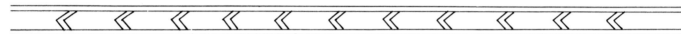

EMBROIDERY HOOPS AND FRAMES

The Turkish embroidery technique requires the use of both hands. So, the largest piece of equipment one needs is a standing hoop or frame set, sometimes called a needle easel. They are available in the United States in many different types, such as hand, table, and floor frames with different tape lengths, and completely adjustable for the height and angle to accommodate any sitting position. (See Sources of Supply at the end of the book for these frames as well as other materials mentioned in this chapter.)

THREADS

The richness of Turkish embroidery does not only come from the elegant patterns but also from the use of gold and silver threads. These must be thin and flexible, and are used in two forms, round and flat. The round DMC one-ply gold and silver threads, technically called *lamé*, available in the United States from fine stitchery shops, are acceptable for Turkish embroidery although the threads traditionally used are thinner and of a finer quality, and can sometimes be obtained from Suppliers under the name of *filé*. As you will see in the photographs in the following chapters, gold and silver threads are always used in many plies to provide a rich effect, so that the extra thickness is not a disadvantage. There are thicker prepackaged metallic gold and silver threads, sometimes three-ply, available in some needlework departments and crafts shops. These can be used for making *kordon* (see Chapter 3) when they do not clash with gold and silver threads already used on the same piece. Flat metallic thread (sometimes called *plate* or *tinsel*) is more difficult to obtain, although it can be gotten in some needlework shops and from thread suppliers. Flat threads have a shiny surface. They fill in a pattern quickly and provide richness for the design. In the event they are not available, do not be discouraged, for you can always substitute round gold or silver thread. Although the effect of the pattern and stitch will be different, the result will be as good.

Turkish embroidery traditionally uses silk threads, which are expensive and hard to obtain in the United States since they are imported. However, it is worth the effort to try to obtain them since silk gives a muted lustrous tonal effect that cannot be exactly duplicated by any other thread. Rayon thread, as shown in the color swatches by Springer Marlitt in color picture c-7, is a good substitute for silk in luster and tone. The color numbers marked on the pattern in this book refer to the Springer Marlitt color swatches. Of course you can use other brands as well, as long as you know the colors referred to on a pattern.

The combination of pastel colors, either silk or rayon, and gold and silver threads yields stunning results in tablecloths and placemats. Bolder colors have been used in Turkish embroidery also, having been introduced in the last century. Some contemporary workers even use orlon wool to embroider on woolen material or leather.

NEEDLES

For silk, rayon, and round metallic threads you will need ordinary sewing needles. For the flat gold or silver threads, crewel needles may be used, since any sharp needle with a large eye is appropriate.

MATERIALS

Turkish women have applied their embroidery to all kinds of garments, including boots, and all sorts of cloths to decorate their homes. The court embroidery was traditionally done on costly matrials such as silk, velvet, and fine linen, but many various types of fabric can be used. There is no limit to the choice of material. You can use manufactured linen, satin, gauze, silk, leather and wool for garments, which are usually embroidered in stitches that do not require the counting of threads and are worked in fancy designs within the outline of a transferred pattern.

For tablecloths, placemats, handkerchiefs, sashes, and belts, where counted-thread patterns in more classical designs are used, your best choice is handwoven linen with a slightly loose weave. When the material is not too fine or tightly woven it is easier and faster to work on it.

HOW TO TRANSFER DESIGNS

Draw a pattern with a pencil on a piece of thin paper such as tracing paper or the tissue paper used in sewing patterns. If tracing paper is used, you can take the pattern directly from one of the clearly reproduced drawings throughout this book.

Then prick holes in the lines of the pattern with a sewing needle. To make it easier, you can mount the needle on an old watercolor brush to hold it more steadily. The job of perforating can be made more efficient by using a small tracing wheel that looks like a cowboy's spur. These are available from art supply stores, where they may be called "pounce wheels," or are available prepackaged in sewing notions departments.

After perforating the whole pattern, turn it face down on the material you are going to embroider and secure it with pins. In Turkey the pattern is then transferred to the cloth by working powdered charcoal, which has been wrapped in gauze, into the holes on the paper. Where powdered charcoal is not available, a piece of artist's charcoal or pastel may be crushed to powder and then put into the piece of gauze so that it forms a small ball. When transferring to dark cloth you can use ordinary talcum powder. The gauze ball is then knocked or "pounced" softly on the pattern so that the powder falls through the holes.

After pouncing, lift the paper and you will see small dots of powder on the cloth in the outline of the design. These dots must be connected by fine lines in a light or dark color depending on the shade of the background material. After the lines have been drawn in you can wipe off the charcoal with a tissue. For drawing the lines it is preferable to use watercolors with a fine brush, but in the event that you are clumsy with a brush you can use a pencil—but only with the lightest touch. Both charcoal and watercolor are washable. Therefore, you can correct errors and there will be no smudges on your embroidery.

2-1. Design transferred from paper to material, with some of the dots of charcoal already connected by a fine watercolor line.

2-2. Drawing of the transferred design.

13

HOW TO ENLARGE OR REDUCE A PATTERN

When you need to change the size of a pattern, as for instance when you have copied a small drawing from this book and want to use it as a large motif on a garment, it can be done simply and quickly with a grid system. First divide the small pattern into a convenient number of squares of equal dimension, and number them vertically and horizontally as shown in the illustration. Next, set up a grid system for the size you want the new pattern to be.

You can do this in two ways—either find the proportion of enlargement and draw each square that many times as big or divide the new width of the pattern into the same number of boxes as the old width, which automatically enlarges each square to your proportion. No matter how you make your new grid, it must have the same number of boxes vertically and horizontally as the old grid, and each box must again be square. Remember to draw your new grid on paper suitable for perforating with a needle so that the enlarged pattern to be drawn in the grid can eventually be transferred to cloth.

To draw the pattern in the new grid, make the same slants, lines, curves and shapes in the correspondingly numbered box on the new grid, enlarging them so that they look as similar as possible to the small pattern. To reduce a pattern, follow the same steps on a grid of smaller rather than larger proportions. No matter whether you are enlarging or reducing, divide small and intricate patterns into a larger number of boxes so that each square has the minimum number of details for transferring. If only a small part of the pattern is complicated, you can make a finer grid within one of the squares of the more open grid and transfer it in the same way.

To enlarge or reduce a pattern based on counting threads for the stitches, one must merely change the number of threads over which the stitches are worked, making sure that both the horizontal and vertical dimensions are enlarged or reduced in the same relative proportions so that the appearance of the pattern is not altered.

2-3. A floral design.

2-4 and 2-5. Steps in enlarging the floral pattern by a grid system.

14

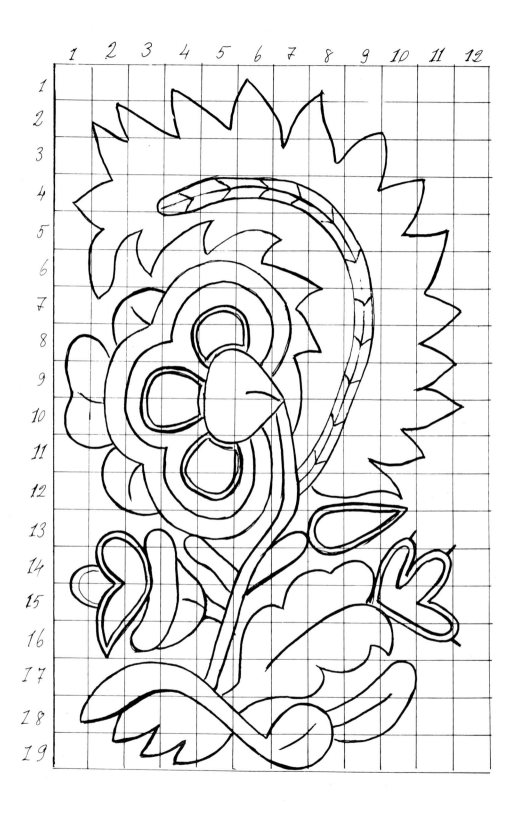

15

3 Stitching Techniques for Turkish Embroidery

Turkish embroidery has a glamorous look because of its gold and silver threads, its highly artistic and original designs, and its meticulous workmanship. There are almost thirty-five different stitches which can be combined in a great number of ways. The most commonly used stitches and their variations are presented here for you to practice before you go on to learn about the color combinations and the use of the stitches on daily wares, articles for decorating your home, garments and accessories, and gifts for your friends.

The stitches fall into two categries, those which are made within the marked outline of a design (*sarma, puan, balik sirti, sira* variations, *gözeme* variations, *kordon, atki, lokum*) and those which are made over a counted number of threads (*pesent, mürver, mushabak, civankashi, kesme,* and *susma*).

SARMA

Sarma is one of the easiest and most frequently used Turkish stitches. It is quite similar to satin stitch.

Work from left to right. Bring the needle and thread out on the left side of the pattern and insert it on the right side. The movement of the needle should always be clockwise. The stitches should be worked close together side by side. Care should be taken to create a neat line along the edges of the shape being filled.

Sarma can be worked straight in a variation called *düz sarma* or on the slant in a variation called *verev sarma*. You will have to decide which one to use. The slanted stitch has more possibility for movement. Stripes, centers of the floral designs, and small leaves are the motifs most frequently done with *sarma* stitch. In general, it is used to cover narrow stripes and small areas.

It can be flat or raised. For a raised effect, it is padded with a running stitch in cotton thread (picture 3-3).

If a pattern has stitches in different directions, to obtain a neat result and smooth transfers from straight

to slanted *sarma* or vice versa, the slanted and straight stitches should be marked on a design drawn on paper, as seen in the samples in Chapter 4. If the result is not good, you can always erase it and start again. But when you embroider, to have to rip out the work to correct an error is quite discouraging. Sometimes even the angles of the slanted stitches must vary to obtain a smooth finishing (picture 3-3).

Puan

Puan is a small circular shape which is filled with *sarma* stitch in any direction as is seen in the Index of Stitches at the end of this chapter. *Puan* is a very commonly used design and stitch in Turkish embroidery.

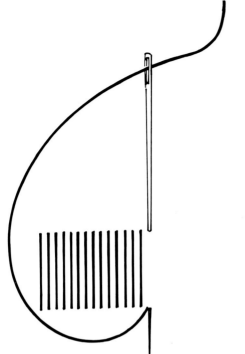

3-1. How to embroider *sarma* stitch.

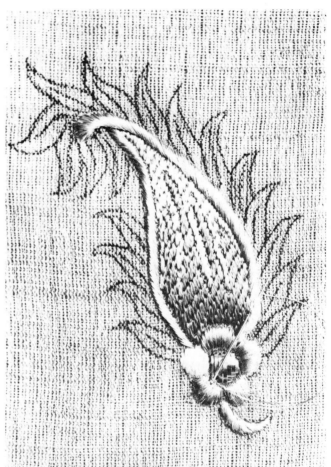

3-3. Padded *sarma* stitch, showing straight *sarma* in the flower and diagonal *sarma* in the almond shape. A careful working of the angles of the slanted *sarma* obtains a finished effect on the curled tip.

3-2. *Sarma* stitch.

BALIK SIRTI (FISHBONE STITCH)

This common stitch is quite simple to make, and goes very fast. Wide stripes, border lines, small leaves, floral designs and small areas can be filled with *balik sirti.*

Bring out the needle and thread at A, insert at B, and then come up on the center line at A. From A, bring the needle out at C, following a diagonal slant. From C, reinsert the needle at the center line meeting the point of the first half of the stitch (picture 3-4). *Balik sirti* can be described as a succession of V's. It is principally embroidered upwards, but there is no reason why you should not do it downwards as seen on the sample (picture 3-5). Whether upwards or downwards, always work from the edges to the center line.

When you see unfinished center lines in the drawings given in this book, it indicates the spine of the fishbone stitch, showing that they must be filled with *balik sirti,* as seen in the leaves and centers of picture 4-4 in Chapter 4.

Usually *balik sirti* is worked close together, but whenever necessary it can be embroidered in a spaced variation, with distance between each stitch.

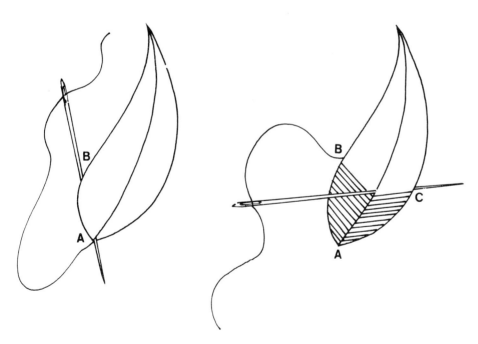

3-4.   How to embroider *balik sirti* stitch.

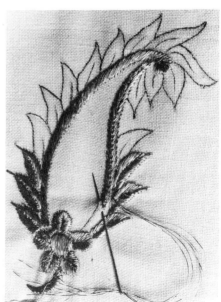

3-5. *Balik sirti* stitch, worked downwards.

SIRA VARIATIONS
Sira ishi (double sira)

Sira ishi technique is quite similar to double running stitch. A row of running stitches of equal length with equal space is worked. Although you do not necessarily count the stitches, try to make stitches of equal length. The only difference in technique from running stitch is the fact that the needle comes from the back to the front with its eyed section. This way, the pointed end does not catch the material. The gaps are filled when going back by inserting the needle in exactly the same holes as the first row.

Sira ishi is quite frequently used to fill large areas. It has some variations.

Verev sira (diagonal sira)

After completing one row of *sira ishi* (picture 3-6), you either drop or go up one or two threads. Start close to the first row and repeat the same movements (pictures 3-6 and 3-7). *Verev sira* is sewn with vertical stitches, but the end result has the look of diagonal stripes. This stitch is also referred to as *sik sira*, meaning "worked close together," or simply as *sira ishi*. When, later in this book, the stitches of a design are described as *sira ishi*, you will decide for yourself which is most appropriate.

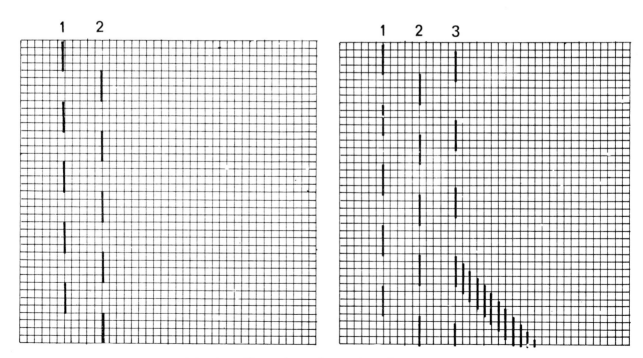

3-6 and 3-7. First and second steps of *sira ishi*.

Düz sira (straight sira)

It is sewn with straight vertical stitches and is worked close together. It has no sloping directions.

Seyrek sira (spaced sira)

Seyrek sira is worked with a space between the row of stitches, and it has a lighter effect than *sira ishi* worked close together.

3-8. How to embroider *düz sira*. The dotted lines indicate stitches on the reverse side of the cloth.

3-9. How to embroider *seyrek sira*. The dotted lines indicate stitches on the reverse side of the cloth.

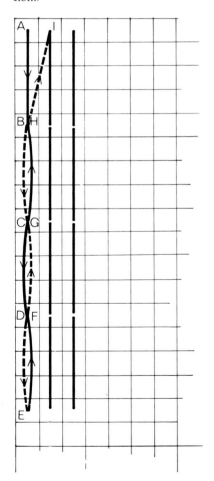

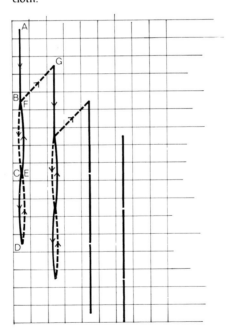

3-10. *Seyrek sira.*

20

Shekline göre sira
This variation follows the outline of
the pattern. When you use this technique, you have to draw the stitches
on the paper pattern first to see
which way you get the best result,
as shown in the illustrations in
Chapter 4.

Döne döne sira (circular sira)
It follows circular lines. It starts from
the center of the circular design and
works towards the outside. You see
in picture 3-12 all the above-
indicated *sira ishi* stitches.

3-11. *Shekline göre sira.*

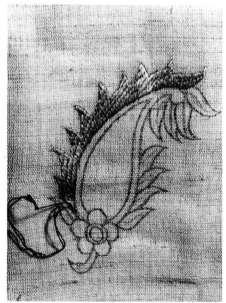

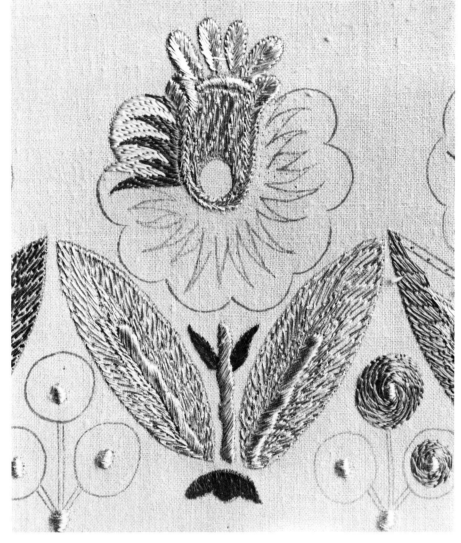

3-12. Several varieties of *sira ishi* stitch. *Döne
döne sira* is worked in the flower at lower right.

PESENT

This stitch is one of the oldest in the Turkish embroidery. *Pesent* is the counted *sira ishi*. Usually four threads of the ground fabric are counted for every stitch. However, in the sixteenth century some very fine garments and Sultans' kaftans (picture c-1) were embroidered by using *pesent* counted over three or even two threads for each stitch. As you can see in the sixteenth-century *bohcha* in picture c-9, such fine embroidery looks like a woven textile.

GOZEME

Gözeme is the stitch used for outlining a design or for marking a dividing line within an area. The technique is the same as *sira ishi*, but the outlining is always done after the area is fully embroidered.

Gözeme is one of the essential stitches of Turkish embroidery. While bringing out the pattern, it gives a neat finishing to a design. You will notice the difference before and after outlining a pattern. In general, *gözeme* is embroidered with a darker shade of the color used in the area to be outlined or with gold and silver thread. A most common shade for *gözeme* is a color called *chitak*, which is a rich dark brown (thread number 1071 in color picture c-7).

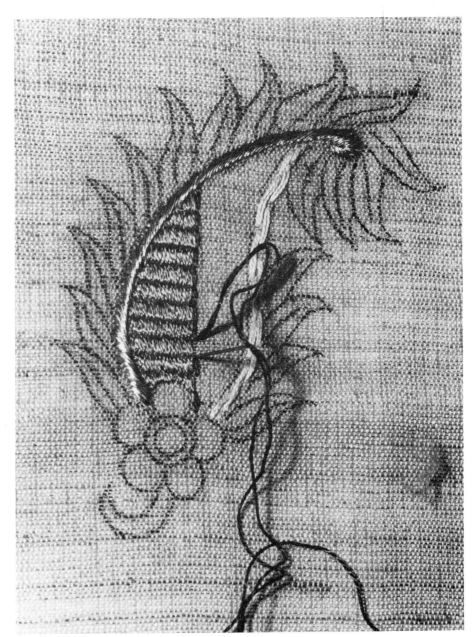

3-13. *Pesent.*

Gidip gelme gözeme

Gidip gelme gözeme (two-way outlining) is worked as a *single* row of *sira ishi*. A row of *sira ishi* is made by working in two directions (see picture 3-9), hence the name. The embroidery in picture 4-5 has a very distinctive *gidip gelme gözeme* outlining.

Dish dish gözeme

Dish dish gözeme (tooth-like gözeme) is like one row of *seyrek sira*, with one thread of the ground fabric between each stitch. This variation is shown clearly in the upper part of picture 3-14 and in pictures 5-3 and 5-5.

Chift gözeme

Chift gözeme (double *gözeme*) is created when there are two rows of *sira ishi* worked close together, as clearly illustrated in the stems in picture 5-5. In the latter part of the book, outlining will be referred to simply as *gözeme*. It is up to you to decide which one of the three outlining stitches to use.

3-14. Three types of *gözeme*.

KORDON

Contemporary fashions use bolder designs than traditional ones, and in keeping with the fashion of the day, Turkish embroidery becomes fancier and bolder when applied to contemporary garments. *Kordon* is used only on garments as an outlining and a filling stitch (pictures 3-15 and 9-4).

You can either make your own thread for *kordon* or buy it ready made. Several plies of thin gold, silver, or silk thread are twisted to obtain a heavy thread for making *kordon*. Although multiple strands of thin threads are preferable, some of the heavier metallic thread that can be bought prepackaged can be used. Springer Bella Donna rayon threads are thick enough to be used for *kordon* when necessary, without twisting several plies, as done with silk or gold threads.

The thickness of the twisted thread is decided according to the material it is used on and to the size of the loops of *kordon*.

3-15. *Kordon* as outlining and filling stitch.

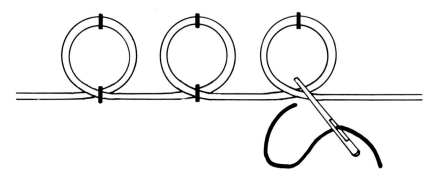

3-16. How to make *kordon*.

For *kordon* outlining, a circular loop of thread is made by hand and placed on the material while one ply of the same color thread is used in small stitches to anchor the loop down on the material (picture 3-16). Two, three, or more stitches are made depending on the size of the loop (picture 3-17). *Kordon* can be applied on a woolen material or other thick fabrics by using correspondingly thicker thread or yarn.

Döne döne kordon (circular kordon)
When used as a filling stitch, mostly in circular and oval centers of motifs, the twisted thread is spiraled without making loops (picture 3-18), and the rounds of yarn are tacked down with small stitches in a technique very similar to couching.

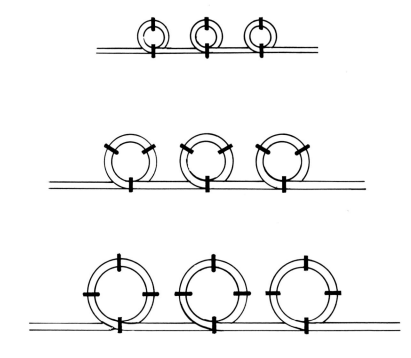

3-17. How to anchor various sizes of *kordon*.

3-18. How to make *döne döne kordon*.

25

ATKI

Atki is mostly used to fill in large centers of flowers. It is a stitch made in several layers. First threads are laid across the shape horizontally. Then another set is laid across them vertically without interlacing. Finally the stitch is secured with regular cross-stitches in a contrasting color. Picture 3-19 shows flat metallic thread secured with contrasting stitches. Several plies of round metallic thread or silk might also be used, and the cross-stitches could be in the same color.

Threads can also be laid across the shape in a diagonal grid. In that case, the intersections are secured with horizontal and vertical cross-stitches (picture 3-20).

3-19. *Atki* stitch with horizontal and vertical threads as ground.

3-20. *Atki* with diagonal threads as ground.

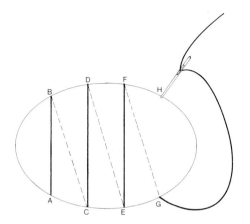

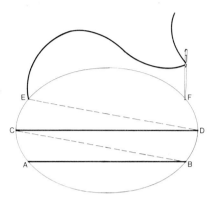

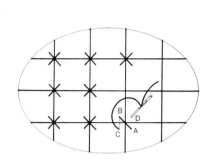

3-21, 3-22 and 3-23. Three steps in making *atki*. The horizontal and vertical grid with diagonal cross-stitches is shown, but the same principles apply to a diagonal grid.

3-24. Drawing of a design with stitches marked for an *atki* center.

LOKUM

Lokum is quite similar to basket-filling stitch (picture 3-25). It is used to fill in rather large central areas. It is worked in alternate groups of four or five horizontal and vertical *sarma* stitches (see picture 3-2). The number of stitches and the size of the squares can be decided according to the thickness of the thread and the size of the pattern. There are four kinds of *lokum*—flat, flat and outlined, padded, and padded and outlined.

It may be interesting for you to know that *lokum* takes its name from the world-famous confection, Turkish delight. Although it is a traditional stitch, it can easily be adapted to heavier work. You might use *lokum* stitch with multicolor yarn to embroider cushions.

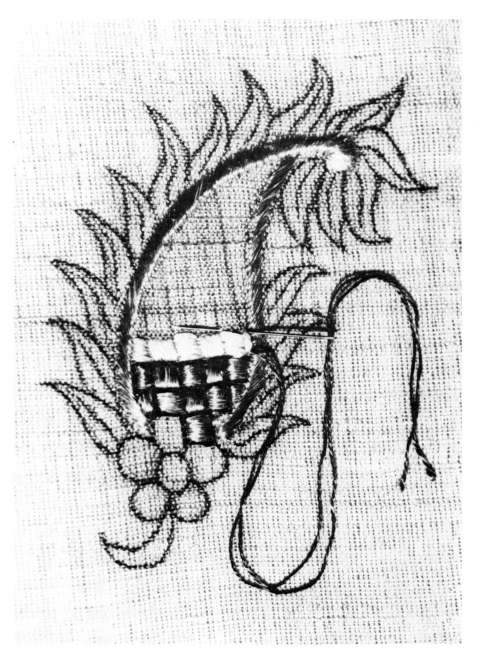

3-25. *Lokum*, padded and outlined.

MÜRVER

Mürver is a counted stitch not widely used but good for filling large centers of floral designs (picture 3–26). Generally the horizontal stitches are made over double the number of threads used for the vertical ones. On fine cotton, six and three threads respectively are recommended; however, the number of threads counted depends on the material used. There is no reason why you should not use this stitch on heavy material with yarn to make some household items such as curtains, bedspreads, and so on.

3-27. Detail of embroidered *mürver*.

3-26. *Mürver* as a filling stitch.

The first step is worked from left to right in a generally upwards direction. Bring the needle and thread out at A. Insert the needle at B. Come out at C. Insert the needle at D, going over the stitch formed between A and B, and bringing the needle out at E. Insert the needle at F, and bring it out again at B. Insert the needle at G over the stitch between E and F, and so on (picture 3-28).

When you go up all the way to the end of the shape, start going down to complete the cross shapes (picture 3-30). For this second step, insert the needle at G. Come out at F. Insert it at E, come out at H, insert at G, and come out at B. Insert the needle at A, come out at E, insert at D, come out at C (picture 3-31). Although this stitch seems complicated it becomes easier with practice and gives a regular pattern where the vertical lines are single while the horizontal ones are double. The vertical stitches always go in the same hole in between the horizontal stitches, as clearly seen in picture 3-27.

3-28. How to make the first step of *mürver*. The dotted lines indicate stitches on the reverse of the fabric.

3-29. Diagram of the completed first step of *mürver*.

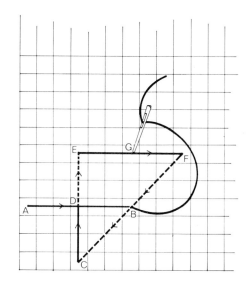

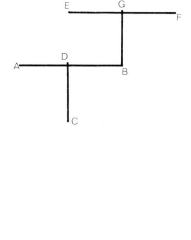

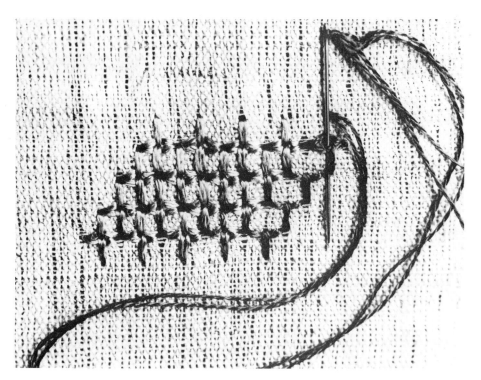

3-30. Second step of *mürver*.

3-31. How to make the second step of *mürver*. The lines that do not have arrows indicate stitches made in the first step of *mürver*.

3-32. Diagram of the completed second step of *mürver*.

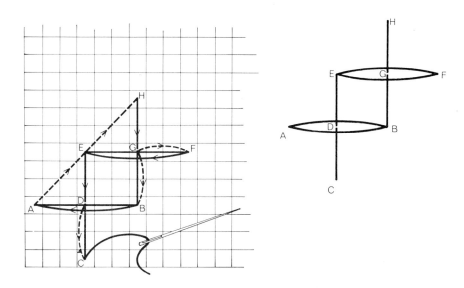

MUSHABAK

Mushabak is also a counted stitch which is not used frequently in today's Turkish embroidery. Usually it is worked to fill large central areas (picture 3-33). It is a simple stitch to make. The number of threads counted on ground fabric varies according to the material used. On a fine cotton, count four threads vertically and six threads horizontally. This stitch too can be used on cushions, curtains, and table mats when embroidered with yarn in big stitches. With cheerful colors very good results can be obtained.

The first step is worked from left to right in an upward direction. Bring the needle and thread out at A. Insert the needle at B. Come out at C. Insert it at D, and bring it out at B. Insert the needle at E, bringing it out at D. Insert it at F, and bring it out at E, and so on (picture 3-35). The result is two slanted parallel lines (picture 3-36).

For the second step start working downwards. Insert the needle that came out at E, at F, and then bring it out at D. Insert at E and come out at B. Insert at D and come out at C. Insert the needle at B, come out at A, insert at C to complete the shape (picture 3-38). On this second step horizontal and reverse diagonal lines are formed between the two slanted parallel lines previously made (picture 3-39). The reversed side of the material is also embroidered the same way.

When starting a second row, start from C and go in and out at D, F, and so on. *Mushabak* has double slanted lines, while the horizontal and vertical lines are single.

3-33. *Mushabak* as a filling stitch.

3-34. Detail of the first step of *mushabak*.

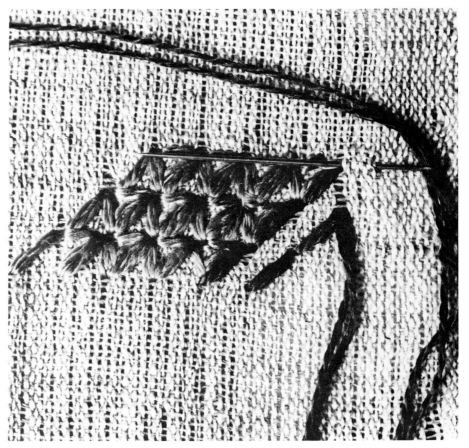

3-35. How to embroider first step of *mushabak*.

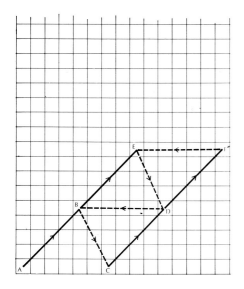

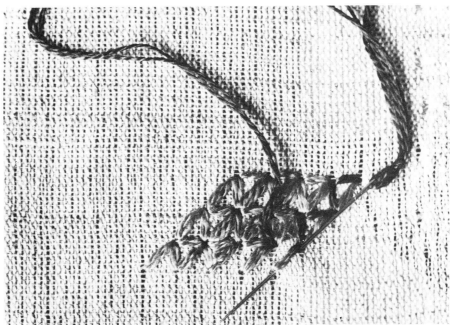

3-37. Detail of the second step of *mushabak*.

3-36. Diagram of the completed first step of *mushabak*.

3-38. How to embroider the second step of *mushabak*. The lines that do not have arrows indicate stitches made in the first step.

3-39. Diagrams of the completed second step of *mushabak*.

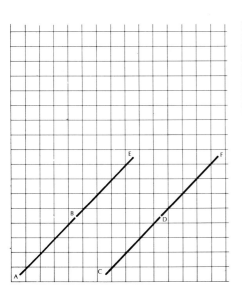

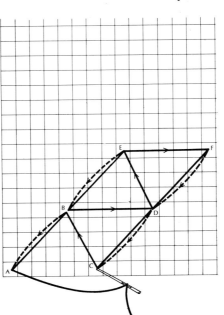

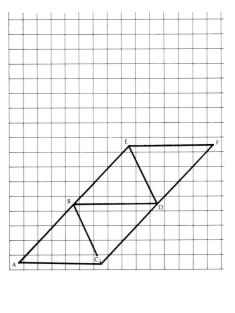

KESME

Kesme is not used very often in Turkish embroidery and resembles drawn threadwork with needle weaving. It can be worked on table mats, tablecloths, shirts and dresses, if desired. It is a rewarding stitch to use for creating your own design, but be sure to practice it on a sampler before starting to embroider it.

The first step in *kesme* is to frame the area to be embroidered, as seen in the upper part of picture 3-40. The framing stitch is called *antika* and is worked from left to right. Bring the needle and thread out at A. Insert the needle at B. Come out at C, go in at D, come out again at B, and go in at D. Begin again by coming out at E, and so on. Work this into a closed rectangular frame of stitches.

After the framing is done, cut the horizontal threads of the cloth you are embroidering, on both ends within the frame. Pull the threads out of the cloth. Now you are left with vertical threads only. Then, according to a pattern you have previously decided, weave the needle and thread under and over these vertical threads of the ground stitches as shown in the bottom part of picture 3-40. Reverse directions and weave back and forth until the frame is filled. Be sure that you count the threads to obtain a regular pattern.

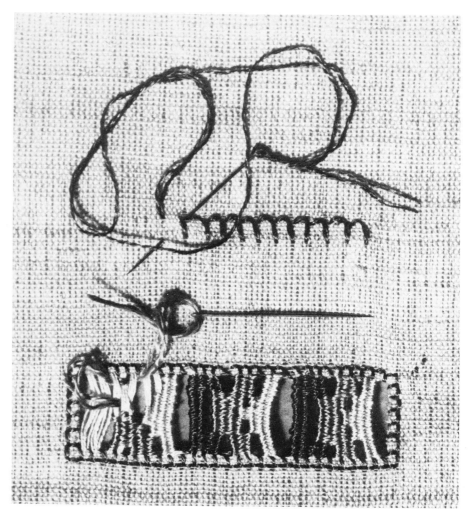

3-40. *Kesme.*

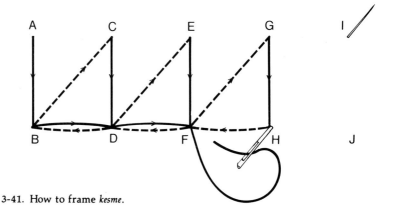

3-41. How to frame *kesme.*

34

SUSMA

Susma follows the *sarma* stitch technique (see picture 3-1). Although it is a stitch mainly for borders, an imaginative person can create innumerable designs by using *susma* stitch in various color combinations. Cushions, curtains, lampshades, bedspreads, table mats can be embroidered with this stitch in addition to applications on a dress or shirt.

It is worked from left to right in horizontal stitches and the rows move diagonally upwards. Bring the needle and thread out at A, insert it at B, come out at C, and so on. As seen in picture 3-43, after four even stitches the needle comes out in the center of the stitch formed between G and H, and a new set of four stitches begins at that point.

The second diagonal row starts from the bottom, and the needle comes out successively at B, D, F, H, and so on. Every new row works upwards.

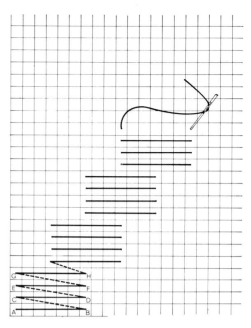

3-42. *Susma.*

3-43. How to make *susma* stitch.

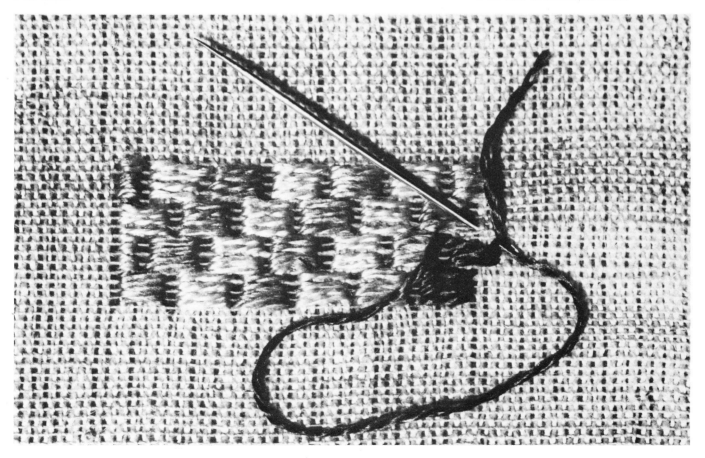

Üchgen Susma

Üchgen susma (triangle susma) is worked with vertical sarma stitch (picture 3–44). It starts by coming out and going in over one thread of the ground fabric, the next stitch worked is over two threads and so on, until a triangle shape is formed. Always work from left to right.

By playing around with several rows of triangle susma border, different designs can be created. For example, a row of triangles may meet with another either on the straight line of the base or on the pointed end. In the latter case empty diamond shapes are formed between the two rows, which can be filled with diagonal sarma stitch.

3-44. Üchgen susma.

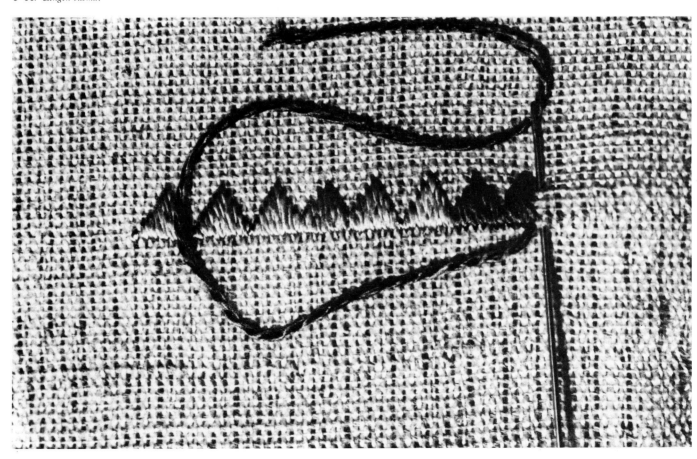

CIVANKASHI

Civankashi is a stitch that is worked in *sarma* technique by counting the threads of the ground fabric. To those familiar with needlepoint, it is very similar to the popular bargello stitch, although it is made in a different sequence. The first step is to embroider the inner triangles (picture 3-45) which are spaced *üchgen susma* stitches. Depending on the dimensions of the border, a different amount of space is left between the triangles, and must be counted out carefully beforehand. Then the empty areas between the triangles are filled by embroidering three consecutive rows of *sarma* stitch. Each sarma stitch can be done over two or more threads depending on the design, but they always follow vertical lines. The open area inside the zigzag shape can be filled with little upside-down triangles. With a little imagination, several designs can be created by this stitch.

Civankashi is an elegant stitch just like the meaning of its name in Turkish, "the eyebrow of beauty." However, it works rather slowly and is not used often in modern embroidery.

3-45. *Civankashi.*

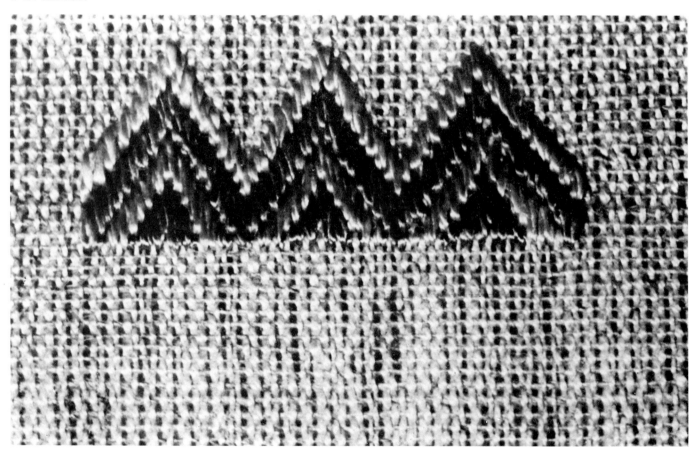

A PICTORIAL INDEX
OF STITCHES

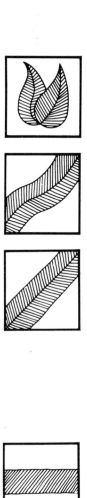

balik sirti

verev sarma

düz sarma

almond shapes worked in **sarma**

puan worked in **sarma**

verev sira

düz sira

seyrek sira

shekline göre sira

sira ishi in two colors

döne döne sira

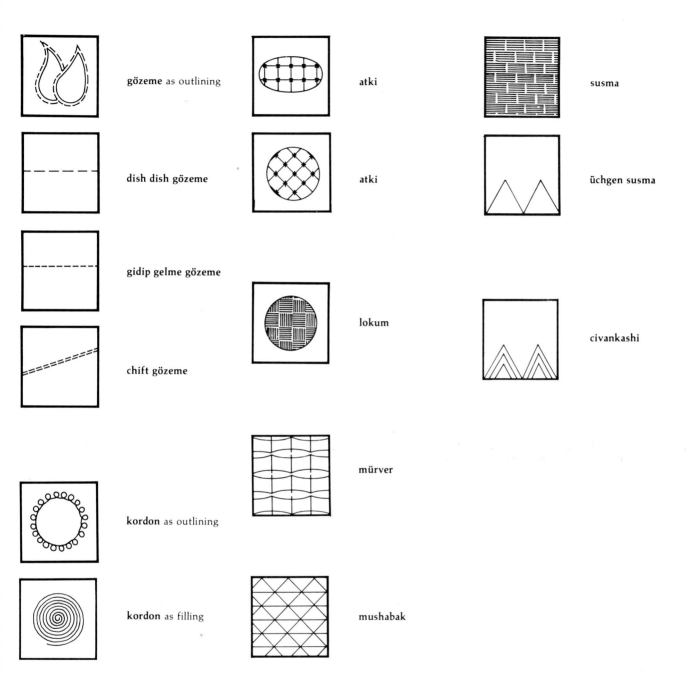

gözeme as outlining

dish dish gözeme

gidip gelme gözeme

chift gözeme

kordon as outlining

kordon as filling

atki

atki

lokum

mürver

mushabak

susma

üchgen susma

civankashi

4 Choosing the Right Stitch for a Design

The most commonly used stitches in Turkish embroidery today are *sira ishi*, *sarma*, *balik sirti*, *gözeme*, and *kordon*. A brief summary of where to apply these stitches will be useful as a reference when you begin to follow the patterns illustrated in this book or to create your own.

Sira Ishi

This stitch is used very extensively in all its variations. The large petals of flowers are usually filled with some form of *sira ishi* and it is used to embroider big leaves, large areas, and shapes with complicated outlines.

Sarma

Stems and border stripes and the ribs of large leaves (picture 4-1) are generally worked with *sarma* stitch. Stripes of up to one-fifth of an inch can be done with *sarma*. Small leaves, forget-me-nots, *puans* (small circular areas) and almond-shaped leaves are customarily covered with *sarma*.

Balik Sirti

Balik sirti is the stitch for wide stems or stripes and long wide petals of flowers such as tulips. *Balik sirti* can also be used anywhere that *sarma* is used, as long as the shape is wide enough.

Gözeme

As mentioned before, *gözeme* is a type of *sira ishi* used for outlining shapes and creating dividing lines between various stitches or areas of color. Wherever a shape needs a thin outline *gözeme* is used, frequently in a contrasting darker shade or in gold.

Kordon

Kordon is used only on garments, as an outlining stitch where a heavy border is needed, and as a filling stitch within circular areas such as the centers of flowers or on small round fruits and berries.

REFERENCE PHOTOGRAPHS OF STITCHES

The detail photographs in this section indicate various stitches quite clearly. Each is accompanied by an outline drawing, so that you can learn how to interpret the pattern drawings in the book which are not illustrated with photographs and how to draw your own patterns in typical Turkish fashion. Studying these line drawings will make it easy for you to understand their language. For instance, if an unfinished line on a leaf or petal or any other shape has a blunt end, it stands for *gözeme* (inside tulip shape in picture 4-2). If it gets thinner towards the end, it means *balik sirti*. *Sarma* outlinings of the petals are marked with double lines (top of large flower, 4-2). Dividing lines inside the petals indicates *gözeme* (sepals of large flower, 4-2). Sharp zigzag lines stand for the use of two shades of a color worked in *sira ishi* (picture 4-8). Embroidering these designs while referring to the photographs will, no doubt, provide a valuable learning experience for a needleworker who has no background in Turkish embroidery. The Index of Stitches at the end of Chapter 3 should be referred to when it is necessary to refresh your memory about stitch names and variations.

Colors will also be given for each design as guidance. In the floral design in picture 4-1, both shiny gold and flat gold threads are quite obvious. The main flower is pink; the tulip is light pink or white. Small drops are light pink while the leaves are in two shades of green. The three oak-shaped leaves on the stem are blue.

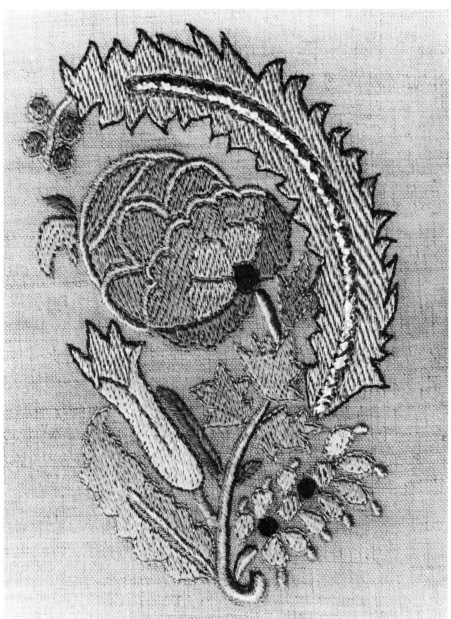

4-1. A floral design embroidered with the most common Turkish stitches.

4-2. Drawing of the floral design.

Picture 4-3 is a typical sample for *gidip gelme gözeme* around the leaves and stems, for double *gözeme* around the flowers, *balik sirti* leaves, and *seyrek sira* petals. The petals are embroidered with a mixture of gold and silk thread of golden color. Mixed colors can be obtained by putting several plies of each color through the eye of a needle. Outlinings are worked with rose-pink thread (number 815, picture c-7) some leaves are gold, while others are green (number 839).

4-3. Sample for single and double *gözeme* and *seyrek sira*.

4-4. Drawing of the *gözeme* and *seyrek sira*.

In picture 4-5, the intermingled stitches of *balik sirti, sira ishi* and *gözeme* are quite obvious. The dark colors are green (number 1033). The leaf on the central stem is blue (number 1053). The top of the trees are worked with silk thread in gold color. The centers of the three star-like flowers are done with flat gold thread and the rest of the design is embroidered with gold thread.

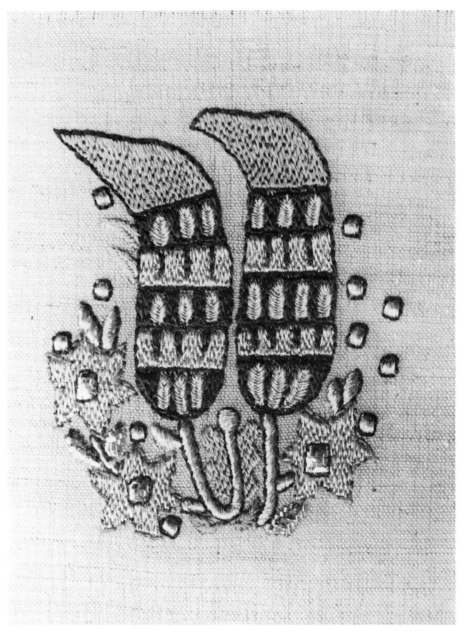

4-5. A stylized tree design.

4-6. Drawing of the tree design.

Balik sirti, sira ishi in two shades and *sarma* outlinings can be seen clearly in picture 4-7. The petals of the round flower are in two shades of blue, the bud pink, the leaves are in two shades of green and the rest is gold. The bud also has two shades of pink. The individual bud is the *serpme* design to be scattered on the table mat. *Serpme* refers to a detail of the major motif, used some distance from the major design area, as shown in examples in Chapter 7.

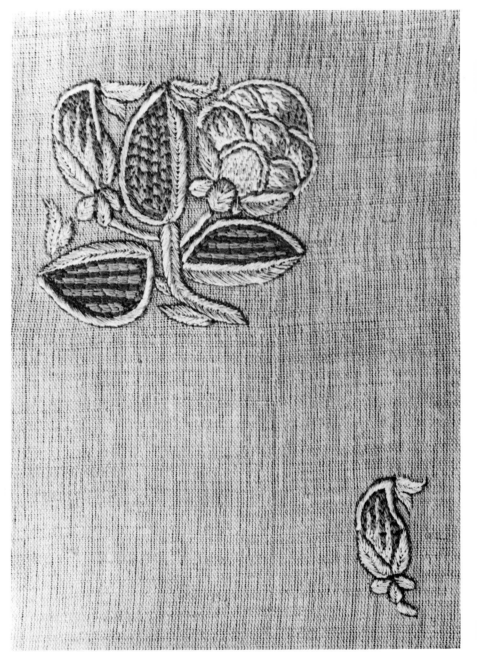

4-7. A floral design for a table mat with *serpme* motif.

4-8. Drawing of the table mat design.

DESIGNS WITH STITCHES MARKED

To obtain a good result in the Turkish embroidery, the angles of the stitches are very important. If not done properly, the pattern would look clumsy rather than smoothly finished. Therefore, it is advisable to draw the stitches of the pattern on the paper. When the result does not look satisfactory, try again. Once the whole pattern is marked, embroidery follows the same angles and directions with ease.

The samples in this section where stitches are marked with give you an idea of what they look like, so you can interpret them, and how they are drawn, so you can draw them in on other patterns. It will be a good practice to embroider these designs also, to learn to follow the marks before trying other patterns, either unmarked or marked by you.

Once again, reference to the Index of Stitches at the end of Chapter 3 will help you remember the traditional markings for each stitch and its variations.

The stitches drawn on the design in picture 4-9 indicate clearly the techniques to be used. Generally, the designs are painted in color indicating all the stitches and color combinations before embroidering. The same practice is strongly recommended to you. In this sample drawing the small leaves are gold, the flowers are two shades of pink, the big leaf adjacent to the stem and the sepals are green. The outlinings are done with a darker shade of green.

4-9. Drawing for a design with all the stitches marked.

4-10. Outline drawing of the same design.

45

A very good sample of use of *balik sirti* stitch is the design in picture 4-11. All stitching is in gold with outlining in brown (number 1071). If silk thread instead of metallic is preferred, 1077 is a suitable golden color. A different shade of the basic color of the background material can also be used with outlining. It is a pretty design for table mats. The number of the repeated designs can be decided according to the size of the mat.

A wide use of *sira ishi* is seen in picture 4-12. These two designs can be embroidered for framing or as table mats. Cushions can be made by enlarging these designs and embroidering heavy material with wool. The motif can also be applied without the circular border to a shirt, dress, or scarf. The carnation is embroidered from the calyx outwards with flat gold thread, gold thread, pink (number 1044) and white (number 800). The tulip is gold with a central leaf embroidered in the pink shade. The stems and the root are gold. The leaves are green (number 839). Hyacinths are white.

4-11. Design and stitch markings for varied uses of *balik sirti* stitch.

4-12. Stylized carnation and tulip designs with stitch markings.

4-13. Outline drawing of the carnation and tulip designs.

Kordon creates a fashionable outline in designs applied to garments. The circular pattern for a dress (picture 4-14) looks richer with *kordon* outlining around the five tulip-like floral designs and all around the frame. The flowers are gold, outlined in brown (number 1071). The almond-shaped designs inside the flowers are worked with flat gold thread surrounded with blue silk thread. The four cloudlike shapes and the very center of the flower are done with flat gold thread.

Picture 4-15 is a sample for the application of *balik sirti* in various directions and for an *atki* center. The areas marked with a star are preferably done with flat gold thread. The rest is in round gold thread. The outlining and the tiny cross stitches of *atki* center are worked in brown (number 1140).

4-14. Circular design for a garment, with stitches marked.

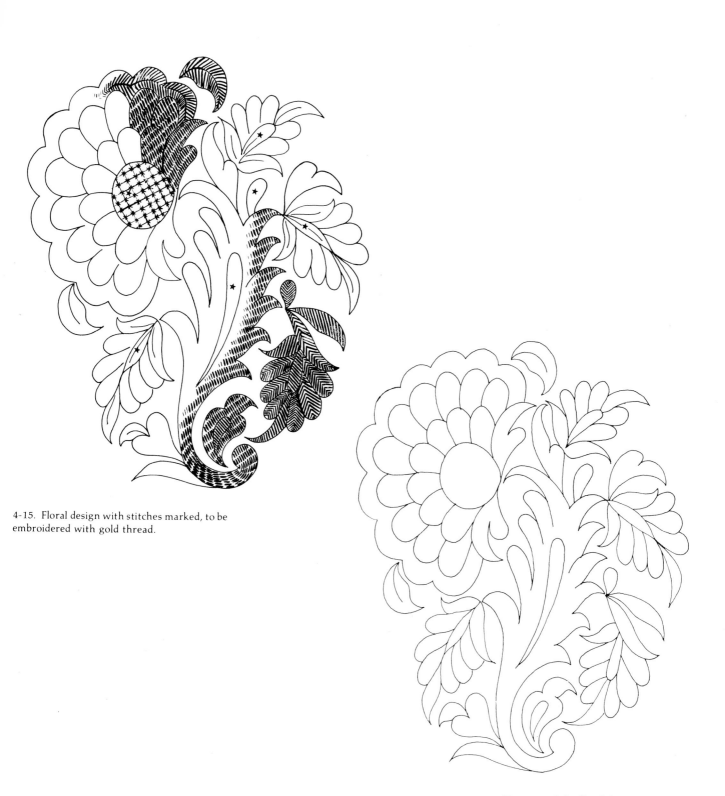

4-15. Floral design with stitches marked, to be embroidered with gold thread.

4-16. Drawing of the floral design.

A floral design (picture 4-17) worked in the most common Turkish stitches *sira ishi, sarma, balik sirti,* and *gözeme,* has typical color distributions as well. The disk is done with flat gold thread. The petal next to it is pink, the second row of petals is gold. The seven outer petals are worked in four shades of pink. The large *sarma* outlinings of the petals are done with gold thread. The leaves are in two shades of green, the three unmarked leaves in the bottom of the vase are also embroidered with gold. The three *balik sirti* leaves at the base of the vase are also done with flat gold thread. The crowning shape is white with a leaf in the center worked with flat gold thread. The stems and the outlining of the vase are in gold. The inside of the vase is blue. The two lower floral designs on each side of the vase are blue with flat gold thread centers, and the two flowers branching out on two sides of the stem are white with gold *gözeme* outlining.

4-17. A design with stitches marked for practicing the most common Turkish stitches and typical color distributions.

5 Colors in Turkish Embroidery

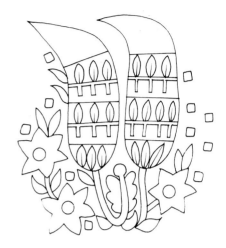

The colors of the threads used in Turkish embroidery are generally muted or pastel shades (see color pictures c-11, c-12, and c-13). The characteristic patterns of classical Turkish embroidery are stylized floral designs, mostly roses, tulips, carnations, hyacinths, forget-me-nots and other decorative patterns, and pink is the most common color for these flowers, while blue is also frequently used. In principle, many shades of pink are used on the petals of a flower to create a natural and artistic appearance. When you see a zigzag dividing line within a petal or a leaf in the drawings in this book, that means two shades of a color, preferably pink, or gold and one shade of a color are to be used (picture c-15.)

As there is a wide range of pink shades, the use of pink never produces monotonous results. The addition of green to the pink petals brings out the design, and therefore sepals or other shapes near the stem are usually done in green or in gold.

Authentic Turkish colors have a much wider range of shades than those shown in color picture c-7 (Springer Marlitt). Silk thread, if available, has the muted appearance and wide range of subtle shades used in Turkish embroidery although the thread is expensive. If you desire to choose the most common shades of pink used in the Turkish embroidery from the Springer Marlitt color swatches, the nearest shades are:

pink: 1213,1019,830,831
      1001,864,1003
      1037,1039,1040
      813,1069,814,863,815
      807,1057,883

When there are big and small flowers on a design, the color used in the big flower is repeated in the small flowers (color picture c-16). Contrasting colors can be added to the small flowers as well. If pink is the color of the major flower, some of the small flowers can be embroidered with blue, yellow, white, or any matching shade of pink.

The large outlines of petals are done with gold thread using the *sarma* stitch. *Gözeme* outlinings are either done with gold, with a contrasting color to the color of the area being outlined, or with brown thread (number 1071), depending on the shade of the petals.

brown: 1011,826,827,1071
       1140,1072

The forget-me-nots are generally in light blue. The inside of flower vases are embroidered with blue outlined in gold or blue thread mixed with gold, silver, or brown (number 1071).

blue: 1052,1053,1055,1056
      1062,803,804,805

The leaves are done with several shades of green and they are outlined with dark green, gold or brown. It is also customary to use gold somewhere on leaves, either fully or partly. Almond-shaped leaves are done alternately with dark and light shades of green or in gold.

green: 1029,1030,1031,1032,1033

869,839,840,1042
1146,1148
1058,810,811,812
832,1066

Gold thread is the most common thread for filling small and large circular areas (color pictures c-15 and c-16). The centers of flowers are also embroidered with gold or flat gold thread. The stems of a flower are almost always in gold or silver although sometimes in brown (number 1071), depending on the color scheme of the design.

Whenever you hesitate to choose a color, it is advisable to use gold thread. That way you can never be wrong, as gold is the most characteristic feature of the classical Turkish embroidery and is used abundantly (color picture c-11) and sometimes solely (color picture c-17) on a design. Following these principles and studying the designs given in this chapter with color keys, color numbers, and color suggestions will enable you to choose your own colors and yet embroider an authentic-looking Turkish design.

5-1. Drawing of the design in color picture c-16.

5-2. Drawing of the design in color picture c-17.

DESIGNS WITH COLOR KEYS

Embroidery is a creative art, and each woman who embroiders is an artist herself and would like to embroider according to her own inspiration. However, practicing a few samples with specifically keyed color instructions may be useful to get oriented to the classical Turkish color schemes.

In the design seen in picture 5-3, gold and silver theads are used together with pink, blue, and green. *Sira ishi* and double *gözeme* stems and outlining with contrast colors are quite clear. It also indicates how *serpme* designs are scattered on a table mat.

✿	1044
○	1033
●	GOLD
⬚	SILVER
✳	803

5-3. A design for a table mat with beautiful *serpme* motif at right.

5-4. Drawing of the table mat design with color key to Springer Marlitt threads shown in color picture c-7.

Picture 5-5 is an excellent example of *verev* (diagonal) *sira*, *dish dish gözeme*, and stems worked in triple *gözeme*. The outlining, or *gözeme*, is done like the first step of *sira ishi*, without going back to fill the gaps. The gaps are actually one thread of the ground fabric. In the stems, *gözeme* is worked like *düz sira*, each stitch following more or less the same length of parallel lines.

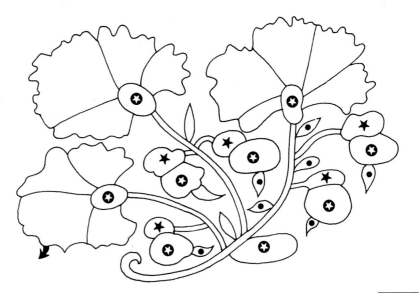

✦	864
↙	1003
•	1011
✪	GOLD

5-5. A sample showing *sira ishi* and *gözeme*.

5-6. Drawing of the *sira ishi* and *gözeme* design, with color key.

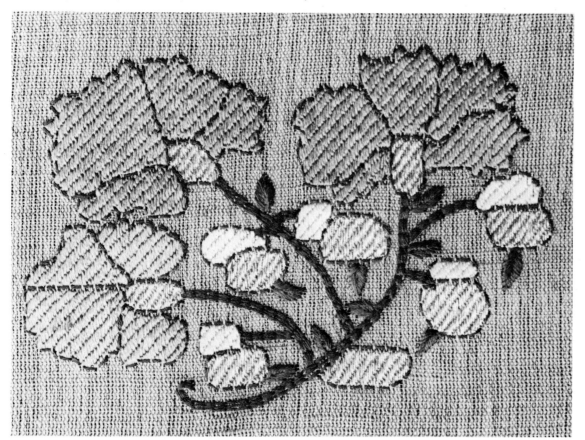

In a multicolor and intricate design (picture 5-7), the stitches are partly marked for guidance. The white, black, and gray shades on the petals are to create the effect of the three shades of pink. The stems and the unmarked areas are embroidered with gold, as is the center of the flower, which is marked to indicate *lokum* stitch.

5-7. An intricate floral design.

826	○
835	□
1003	▼
1011	○
1037	✵
1040	▫
1071	✳
1148	✪
1213	●

5-8. Color key for the floral design.

5-9. An imaginative mind can create a new pattern by using the major part or detail of an intricate design of this sort. This motif can be embroidered on a shirt, dress, scarf, cushion, and so on.

The border of this design is a most commonly used one on table mats. It consists of two parallel lines worked with *sarma* stitch and an area in between filled with *sira ishi*. Such borders can also be applied to garments.

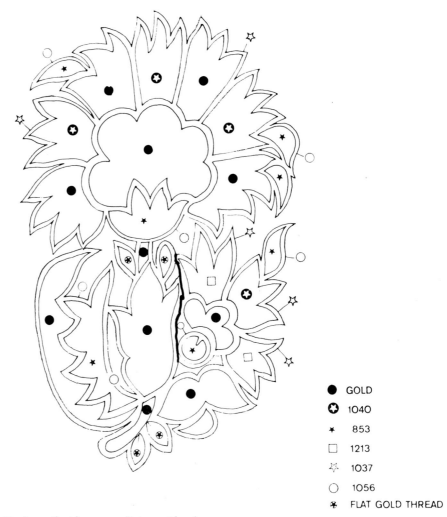

●	GOLD
✪	1040
✶	853
□	1213
✩	1037
○	1056
✳	FLAT GOLD THREAD

5-10. A motif with *sarma* outlining, with color key.

DESIGNS WITH COLOR SUGGESTIONS

After experimenting with some designs which have keys for color, it should not be too difficult for you to follow suggestions for color numbers.

The floral design in picture 5-11 has typical color distributions. In the center of the flower and the almond-shaped drops, flat gold thread is used. In the event it is not available, round gold thread can replace it. The stems, outlinings, and rib of the leaf on the left are made with gold thread. The two sepals are done with light green (number 1029) and outlined with green (number 1033). The inner petals on each side of the disk are embroidered with medium green (1030) and the five petals in between are done alternately with the same shades of green as before (1029 and 1033). On the outer petals six different shades of pink are used (1213, 831, 830, 1019, 1001, 864). Each petal has two different shades of pink. The large leaf is worked with two shades of green (839 and 840). The stacked almond shapes inside the rib of the leaf is gold, and so is the outlining. The grape-like cluster on the left is embroidered with three pinks (1037, 1039 and 1040). For little flowers on the right—the center one is blue (1052) wrapped in gold and outlined with another blue (1055), the two small buds on each side have two shades of pink used before (1213 and 831) with gold stems. The leaves on top of the buds are green (840). For outlining stems and almond drops, *sarma* is the stitch. The rest is done with *sira ishi*. This motif can be repeated horizontally to obtain a large border. It can also be used individually. This sample is typical of the way colors are repeated in Turkish embroidery. Several shades of the main flower's color are repeated in the minor flowers, with the addition of contrasting colors.

5-11. A design with typical color distribution.

57

Some designs can be repeated to make a nice vertical border, and a brocade effect can be obtained by repeating the vertical rows (see historical piece in color picture c-1). The motif in picture 5-12 would be suitable for such an effect. The long leaves are green (869 and 840). Small leaves, stem, V-shapes, and the crowning flourish are gold. The circular designs have three different shades, starting with gold in the center, then blue (1055), and then light blue (1052). The *gözeme* outlining is black. The outer petals are gold, while the ones with V-shapes are dark pink (894) with brown (1072) outlining. The remaining three petals around the one with V-shapes are a lighter pink (1044).

If you wish to embroider something small and simple, try the design in picture 5-13. It would look nice on a blouse or on a dress. Several of the motifs would make a nice vertical border. The forget-me-nots are three pinks (830, 831 and 1213), starting with the darkest shade at the bottom. The *sarma* outlining around the forget-me-nots is gold, and the leaves next to it are green (839). The rest of the design is gold.

If you want to practice the use of several subtly graded shades of a color on a design, embroider the motif in picture 5-14. The center area is done with five shades of green, the darkest shade at the top (from top down: 869, 839, 840, 1029 and 1042). The pointed top part and the circle at the other end are both gold. These five shades of green are separated with gold and pink *gözeme*. The wide outlining is gold *sarma*. The small circular shape at one corner as well as the leaves are gold. The six flower heads are white outlined with gold. The two large circles have a gold

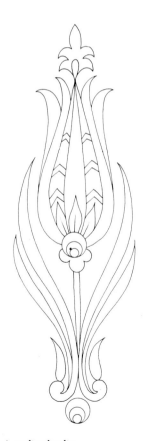

5-12. A stylized tulip.

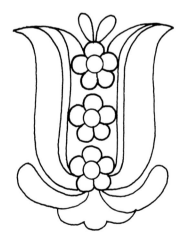

5-13. A small motif for garments.

5-14. A small design.

center, then pink in three shades (1039, 1040 and 1213), with outlining in brown (1072). These circular areas are worked with *döne döne sira*. All the outlines are done with gold, and the almond-shaped stems are also in brown (1072).

A pattern suited for many uses is shown in picture 5-15. These designs can be used as framed hangings, for cushions, for lamp shades, for table mats, and so on. *Seyrek sira* covers the empty areas. The forget-me-nots are blue (1062 or 1053). The petals of the big floral designs are gold, worked in *balik sirti*. Circular and almond-shaped areas are in flat gold thread. *Gözeme* is done with light brown (1140). This design can also be used without its circular frame. This is a good example of how a large design can easily be converted to a small one.

After embroidering some of the preceding designs with specifically designated colors, you should develop a feeling about appropriate Turkish colors and be able to choose the proper shade following the general instructions already given and the general suggestions for each design.

5-15. Motifs for abundant use of *balik sirti* stitch.

Picture 5-16 has also typical color distributions in Turkish embroidery. The petals of the big central flower should be in various shades of pink with green sepals and gold *sarma* outlining. The three crowning flowers are white with *balik sirti* green leaves. The small flowers hanging on both sides are blue. The two bigger flowers on each side of the vase are pink. One of the two flowers next to the stem is blue while the other is white. The vase is blue and gold. The disks, almond shapes, and stems are gold. If the design is to be used on a table mat, there should be borders on both ends of the mat with this floral design repeated as many times as necessary. The small individual *serpme* design shown at the bottom must be scattered in the empty area in the center of the mat.

If you are interested in brocade design, the drawing in picture 5-17 will be a good one to practice. This design can be used individually as well. The carnation in the center should be in two colors, either one color with gold or two shades of one color. The tulips on the curved border are the same color as the carnation; the leaves are green and the rest is gold.

5-16. A design to practice typical color distribution.

5-17. A design that creates a brocade effect
when repeated.

To practice *atki* filling, you can embroider the design in picture 5-18. The center of the flower can be worked with *atki* stitch in gold. Next to the center, dark and light shades of green are used alternately with gold *sarma* outlining. In the next row of petals, the color is two shades of pink. The big petals are pink as are the crowning flowers. The two forget-me-nots are blue. The big leaves are green with gold outlining while the small ones are gold.

In picture 5-19, two shades of pink are used in the large flowers with gold centers and *sarma* outlinings. The small flowers on the stem are white with dark pink centers. The leaves are green with gold *sarma* out-linings. The central design is made with seven shades of green starting with the darkest shade at the bottom. The triple dividing lines in between are *gözeme* with pink and gold. Needless to say, the stems are gold. The individual parallel lines are worked in with flat gold thread.

5-18. A motif with wide use of *sarma* outlining.

5-19. A pattern with pink and white flowers.

A very nice design for a table mat is the drawing in picture 5-20. The petals of the big flowers are worked with pink, the outlining is gold *sarma*. The oval-shaped flowers are blue. The leaves are gold and green. The stems and all the outlinings are gold. The very outermost line of the big flowers is worked with *balik sirti*. The simple border of this table mat can be used on a shirt or a dress as well.

In picture 5-21, you see a design of a stylized carnation. The flower petals are blue. The outlining, the stems, the circular bases of the tulips, and the almond-shaped ribs of the leaves are gold. The leaves are green and the tulips are white. The flower on the right is pink. This design can be repeated to obtain a rich border as well as used individually or two or three times together on each end of a table mat. *Serpme* leaves from the design can be used on a dress or shirt in a scattered fashion to obtain the effect of printed material. Any imaginative person can create several designs from such a single motif.

5-21. A bouquet of carnations and tulips.

5-20. A design for a table mat.

In picture 5-22, the large forget-me-not shape, the stem, the curved stems, and the border around the petal are gold. The central petal is pink, the leaves are green, and every other diamond shape is a color matching with pink and green. The rest of the diamond shapes are gold. The area surrounding the central forget-me-not can be worked with *mürver* or *sira ishi* and the border around the flower with *balik sirti*.

5-22. A round floral design.

Chapter 5 continues on page 73.

c-2. An eighteenth-century Turkish *chevre*. (From the archives of Istanbul Olgunlashma Enstitüsü.)

c-1. Sixteenth-century embroideries on display in Turkish Embroideries Section of Topkapi Palace Museum in Istanbul. (Courtesy of Topkapi Palace Museum.)

c-3. A nineteenth-century Turkish embroidery. (From the archives of Istanbul Olgunlashma Enstitüsü.)

c-4. Copy of the design in the eighteenth-century *chevre* in picture c-2. Drawing of this design is in Chapter 7.

c-5. Design inspired by the nineteenth-century embroidery in picture c-3.

c-6. A nineteenth-century *chevre*. The same pattern was used on an embroidery prepared as a state gift for President Eisenhower. Drawing of this design is in Chapter 7. (From the archives of Istanbul Olgunlashma Enstitüsü.)

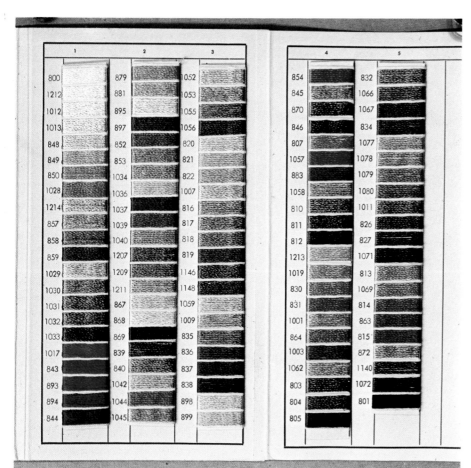

1	2	3	4	5
800	879	1052	854	832
1212	881	1053	845	1066
1012	895	1055	870	1067
1013	897	1056	846	834
848	852	820	807	1077
849	853	821	1057	1078
850	1034	822	883	1079
1028	1036	1007	1058	1080
1214	1037	816	810	1011
857	1039	817	811	826
858	1040	818	812	827
859	1207	819	1213	1071
1029	1209	1146	1019	813
1030	1211	1148	830	1069
1031	867	1059	831	814
1032	868	1009	1001	863
1033	869	835	864	815
1017	839	836	1003	872
843	840	837	1062	1140
893	1042	838	803	1072
894	1044	898	804	801
844	1045	899	805	

c-7. The color swatches of the silk thread made by Springer Marlitt. Color keys for several drawings appear in Chapter 5.

c-8. A sample showing *verev sira* stitch. (See Chapter 3 for other *sira* stitches).

c-9. A sixteenth-century *bohcha* (covering) worked with *pesent* stitch, which is described in chapter 3. (From the archives of Istanbul Olgunlashma Enstitüsü.)

c-10. A hundred and fifty-year-old *chevre* embroidered with *pesent* stitch. (From Nuriye Gürkök Sabuncuoğlu's collections.)

c-11. Color sketch with marked stitches of design indicating Turkish colors and wide use of gold thread, drawn by Nuriye Gürkök Sabuncuoğlu. (From her private archives.)

c-12. Color sketch with marked stitches of design with typical Turkish colors, drawn by Nuriye Gürkök Sabuncuoğlu. (From her private archives.)

c-13. Color sketch of design with marked colors typical of some Turkish embroidery, drawn by Nuriye Gürkök Sabuncuoğlu. (From her private archives.)

68

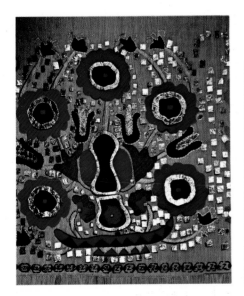

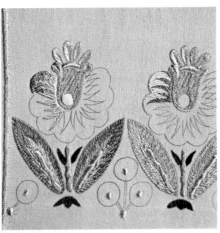

c-14. Color sketch with marked stitches of a primitive floral design in dark colors, brightened mainly by the wide use of flat silver thread, drawn by Nuriye Gürkök Sabuncuoğlu. (From her private archives.)

c-15. A sample of design for a table mat with typical color distribution in Turkish embroidery.

c-16. A sample of typical color distribution in floral designs.

c-17. Color sketch with marked stitches of a design which emphasizes the abundant use of gold thread in Turkish embroidery, drawn by Nuriye Gürkök Sabuncuoğlu. The drawing of this design is in Chapter 5. (From her private archives.)

c-18. Color sketch of a design created by Nuriye Gürkök Sabuncuoğlu after an old towel, drawn by Meral Ishik.

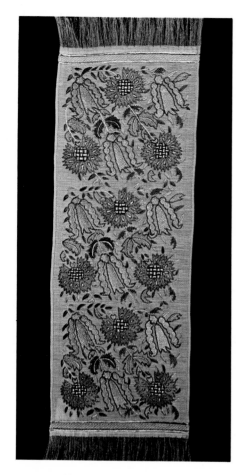

c-20. A table mat. This piece illustrates contrasting color combinations and the use of *gözeme* stitch and fine *sira ishi* stitch (see Chapter 3).

c-19. A table mat. This piece illustrates smooth color combinations and the use of *lokum* stitch (see Chapter 3).

c-21. Color sketch with marked stitches of a tulip design for a dressy garment or an evening gown.

c-22. Color sketch with marked stitches of carnation design to be embroidered on a dress or evening gown.

c-23. Color sketch with marked stitches of the floral design on the short sleeve of an evening gown shown in Chapter 9. This is a good example of the use of pearls in Turkish embroidery. Pearls are sewn in the centers of the grids formed by *atki* stitches (see Chapter 3) and in the centers of the flowers on the border design.

c-24. An elegant evening gown presented by Turkish mannequin Meltem Karapazar. (From the archives of Istanbul Olgunlashma Enstitüsü.)

c-25. Turkish embroidery traditionally follows floral lines. This motif was created and embroidered in Istanbul Olgunlashma Enstitüsü especially for Ayfer Neyzi, who desired a geometric design.

c-26. A pants suit presented by Turkish mannequin Sema German. (From the archives of Istanbul Olgunlashma Enstitüsü.)

YOU DECIDE THE COLOR

After studying the principles of the colors in Turkish embroidery, using given shades, and eventually following suggestions for selection of colors, a creative needleworker will be able to choose her own colors quite easily. This will give more pleasure and confidence in the work and more enthusiasm for finishing it.

Designs in pictures 5-23 through 5-31 are there for you to practice your own colors. The best thing to do is to select the colors and then to put the threads together to see whether they blend well. If not, the shade that does not fit in can be replaced with another one until a harmonious result is obtained.

5-23. This floral design is worked with gold and silver threads, and can be outlined either with a darker shade of the ground fabric or with brown (number 1071). (From the private archives of Nuriye Gürkök Sabuncuoğlu.)

5-24. The repetition of this motif would make a cheerful border. The petals of the big flower are in various shades of pink, and the tulips are white with gold centers. The leaves are green, and *sarma* outlinings are gold. (From Nuriye Gürkök Sabuncuoğlu's private archives.)

5-25. Two shades of pink are used on the petals of the big flower. Small floral designs on both sides are white with green leaves. The crowning flower, the stems, and *gözeme* outlining are gold.

5-26. The round petals of the flower are blue with silver *sarma* outlining. The tulip is pink with gold veins. The stems, circles, and outlining of the leaves are gold. (From Nuriye Gürkök Sabuncuoğlu's private archives.)

5-28. The two big flowers are pink while the smaller ones are white with dark pink disks. *Sarma* outlining, stems, and the disks of the flowers are gold. The central shape is embroidered with gold and several shades of green.

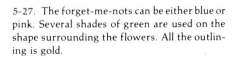

5-27. The forget-me-nots can be either blue or pink. Several shades of green are used on the shape surrounding the flowers. All the outlining is gold.

74

5-29. A design mainly for a table mat. Worked with *sarma, sira ishi,* and *gözeme.* The large centers of the flowers can be filled with *mürver, mushabak, lokum,* or *atki* stitch.

5-30. This design can be framed as a wall-hanging. Enlarged and worked with yarn, the designer can make a very cheerful decoration for a cushion. It can also be applied to garments.

5-31. A typical Turkish motif. It is worked with *sarma, sira ishi,* and *gözeme.* A great variety of colors can be used on this cheerful design. (From Nuriye Gürkök Sabuncuoğlu's private archives.)

6 Designs for Borders

Borders can be very simple when accompanying a floral design or when used alone on a table mat, as seen in the previous chapters. The use of simple borders in various arrangements on garments is also very successful. Repetition of a large and complicated motif produces a rich-looking border, which might be used on a dress near the hemline and on the sleeves or just on the sleeves (see picture 10-5). Borders can be arranged in a few parallel lines as well. An ambitious needleworker can make several creations for dresses, shirts, and skirts by playing around with various arrangements of borders.

Narrow border designs may be embroidered to make headbands or belts, as seen in pictures 6-2, 6-3, and 6-4. A plain dress with a nicely embroidered belt always looks very elegant. Borders may also be used to decorate lampshades, cushions, curtains, bedspreads, and so on.

You can very easily create interesting borders by using a small detail of any design given in this book. Do not forget that sometimes you need to design a small shape to go between the repeated motifs (see pictures 6-2 and 6-3).

With *susma* stitch many interesting and colorful borders can be made. Although not typically Turkish, geometric designs look nice in borders (see picture 10-5). *Sarma* and *sira ishi* are the most common techniques for borders. In the border in picture 6-2, all the areas are worked with gold *sarma*. Petals are in whatever color you choose. Gold or a darker shade of the color used on the petals can be used for outlining. By enlarging one design of this border and using yarn, a pretty cushion can be made.

The border in picture 6-3 is worked with gold thread only. The small circles between the flowers are pearls. The petals and the borders are worked with *sarma*, while the shapes above and below the pearls are embroidered with *sira ishi*. Empty areas do not look nice in Turkish embroidery, and *seyrek sira* is commonly resorted to for dressing up empty areas.

Another example of the use of *seyrek sira* for covering areas where no design is drawn is the border in picture 6-4. In this design, the forget-me-nots are blue, and the inner part of the petals is gold, while the outer part is silver. The rest is gold. The triangle motifs between the circular shapes and the outline are embroidered with *sarma*. One of the floral designs can also be enlarged for making a cushion.

6-1. A design, with stitches marked, that easily adapts itself to a border. It can also be used on mats for coffee tables or end tables and on cushions.

6-2. A border for a headband.

6-4. A border with stylized carnations. It can be used on a headband or a belt.

6-3. A border embroidered in gold with pearls.

6-5. An elegant, simple border for garments.

7 Designs for Table Mats

One of the most frequent applications of Turkish embroidery in household items is to table mats, tablecloths and placemats. Most of the patterns given in Chapters 4 and 5 are originally designs for table mats. However, these designs can also be applied elsewhere.

The oblong table mats are generally designed to have embroidery on both ends as seen in picture 7-1. In table mats, *serpme* designs have several arrangements. A detail of the major patterns is usually scattered on smaller mats meant for end tables (picture 7-1). Tablecloths and placemats have napkins with *serpme* designs. Intricate designs have more detailed *serpme* motifs, as seen in picture 7-7. Depending on the size of the table mat and the design to be embroidered, *serpme* may also be scattered between the motifs on both ends.

7-1. A mat for coffee table with matching mats for end tables.

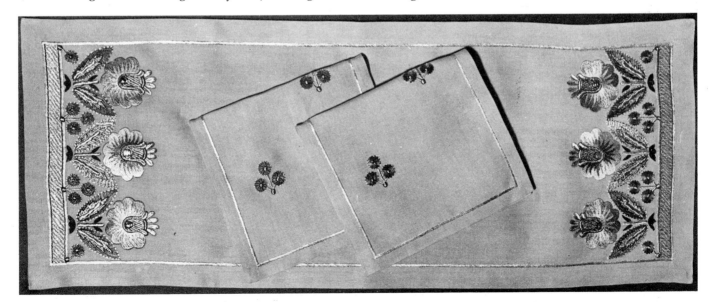

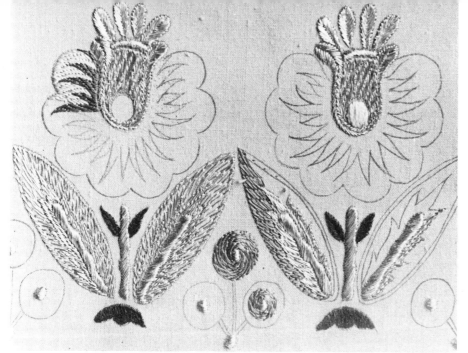

7-2. Detail of the mat while it was being embroidered. This picture is a good reference for all kinds of *sira ishi—verev sira* in the U-shape center of the floral design, *seyrek sira* on the leaves, *döne döne sira* on the circular designs, *shekline göre sira* on the petals, two sizes of padded *puans* (one of the U-shape centers of the flowers, the other in the centers of the three circular shapes placed between the leaves of the two flowers) *balik sirti* leaves, and *verev sarma* stems and ribs of the leaves. After completing the preliminary practice, this might be a good design with which to start Turkish embroidery.

7-3. Detail of another motif of the mat, clearly indicating how a petal with a zigzag dividing line is embroidered with two shades of a color, and how it is done in two steps.

7-4. Drawing of the same design. For the colors, see color picture c-15.

7-5. Center table piece of a set of placemats and napkins.

7-6. Detail of the mat, showing fine *sira ishi*, *lokum*, *sarma*, and *balik sirti* stitches.

7-7. Design for a table mat with a charming *serpme* motif. The central flower is in various shades of pink, the forget-me-nots are in blue, the grapes are in honey color, and the chevron borders are gold with green V's.

Sometimes the same design is repeated throughout the length of a table mat, as seen in color picture c-19. Some table mats have neither designs on both ends nor *serpme*, as seen in the large center piece of a set of place mats in picture 7-5.

If you prefer easy and light embroidery, you can create your own design for table mats, tablecloths, and placemats by using only *serpme* motifs given in Chapters 4 and 5. You can also create your own *serpme* motif inspired from complicated floral designs. There are no strict rules about designing a table mat. Any artistic arrangement would look nice. Be creative, and design your own pattern.

7-8. Design for a table mat. When this design is used as a repeated motif, the additional motif on the left is used on the right side as well to provide a link between the motifs.

7-9. Drawing of the design in color picture c-6.

7-10. Drawing of the design in color picture c-4.

8 Designs for Garments

Although some of the designs given in the previous chapters can be embroidered on garments, the designs in this chapter are generally meant for garments only, and often use pearls and *kordon* for a bold, striking effect.

Actual patterns and line drawings for various types of collars are given for your convenience. They can be enlarged proportionately as explained in Chapter 2, to fit all sizes. A touch of embroidery on collars and cuffs makes a dress look elegant, and a tastefully embroidered buckle (picture 8–9) brings out the stylishness of even a simple outfit.

Before you copy and enlarge a pattern, first decide the colors. Then prepare your paints and mark the stitches in color. When one prepares a design with all the stitches and colors marked, the embroidery produces a perfect result. You can see how your embroidery will look when complete, following the same angles and colors as your sketch. Picture 8-8 shows a marked color sketch very clearly. The shiny almond drops in this picture and circular and oval centers are done with flat gold thread, if available. Round gold thread can easily replace the flat gold thread if need be. The white areas represent gold, and the rest (including outlining) are three shades of blue (1053, 1055 and 1056). You can use three shades of any color you like, or three shades of the color of the ground fabric.

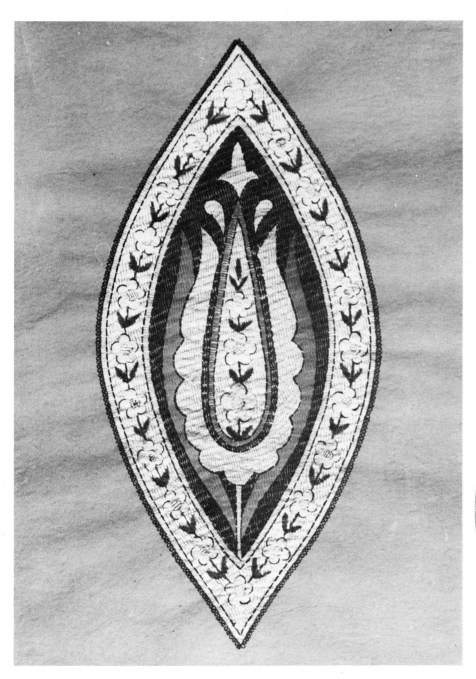

8-1. Marked color sketch of the design seen in
color picture c-21.

8-1a. Drawing of the same design.

8-2. Marked color sketch of the design in color
picture c-22.

8-2a. Drawing of the same design.

84

8-4. This is the design that might be used on the back of the vest. The small circles are pearls.

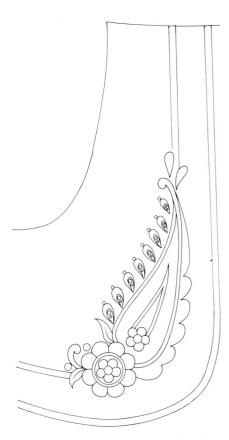

8-3. Design for a vest. To get a bolder effect, it should be outlined with *kordon*. The stitches are *sarma* and *sira ishi*. Several shades of one color and gold should be used.

8-5. This medallion design is worked in gold with the exception of the background area around the forget-me-nots, which is in color. It can be a different shade of the ground fabric or a contrasting color. *Balik sirti*, *sira ishi*, and *sarma* are the stitching techniques. It is a simple but smart pattern for a shirt, dress, or scarf.

8-7. Drawing of the collar design.

8-8. A marked color sketch of a single motif.

8-6. Marked color sketch for a U-neck collar. It is embroidered mainly with gold thread. The centers of the forget-me-nots in the neckline are flat gold thread. *Gözeme* can be any color that goes well with the material of the dress. The outlining is done with gold *kordon*. The oval shapes are joined with a pearl, and a pearl is also used between the petals of the oval floral shape.

8-9. A design for a buckle, to be worked with *sarma* and *sira ishi* in gold.

8-10. A marked color sketch for a collar on a fancy blouse or a dress. The small circular centers should be done with flat gold thread, if available. In the large tear-drop shapes and the area around the circular frame of the forget-me-nots, a different shade of the material of the dress is used. The rest is gold.

8-11. Drawing of the collar design.

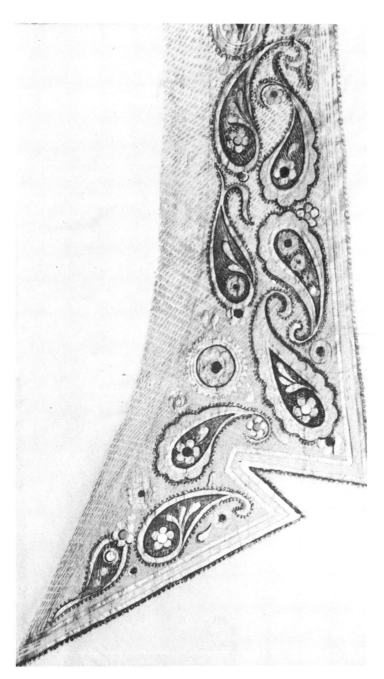

8-12. Marked color sketch for a design for a sports collar. The empty areas are filled with gold worked in *seyrek sira*. Gold and several shades of brown are used. Depending on the color of the material it is embroidered on, the design may be done with various shades of thread. *Kordon* is generally used on this pattern.

8-13. Drawing of the design for the sports collar.

9 Embroidered Garments

In this chapter you will see some elegantly embroidered garments. The drawings of the designs and some close-up photos of step-by-step embroidery will enable you to embroider similar outfits.

9-2. Marked color sketch for the design on the sleeves of the evening gown.

9-1. An embroidered evening gown presented by Turkish mannequin Füsun Ayanoğlu. (From the archives of Istanbul Olgunlashma Enstitüsü; photographed by Teknika Laboratories.)

9-4. Detail of stitchery being worked on the front of the vest. Showing examples of *kordon*, *sarma*, *sik* and *seyrek sira*, *gözeme*, and padded forget-me-nots. The tulips are embroidered alternately with *sik* and *seyrek sira*.

9-3. An evening gown with an embroidered vest, presented by Turkish mannequin Fatosh Altinkum. (From the archives of Istanbul Olgunlashma Enstitüsü; photographed by Teknika Laboratories.)

9-5. Detail of stitchery on the back of the same vest. This shows clearly how the padding is done in opposite direction of *sarma* stitch. One can see how *gözeme* and *kordon* bring out the design.

9-6. Drawing of the borders on the vest.

9-7. Drawing of the design on the sleeves of the vest. The floral design in gold thread is done by working *sarma* stitch in different directions. On such a crowded pattern this produces a smooth result.

9-8. Drawing of the design on the evening gown in picture c-24. The angles of the stitches produce a decorative effect and make the stitching more convenient.

9-9. Marked color sketch of the same motif. The *puans* (circular centers) are in flat gold thread. Gold and several shades of blue are used, the darker shades starting from the center.

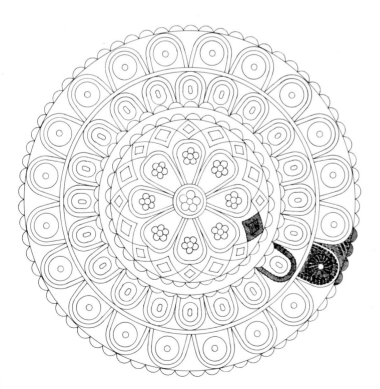

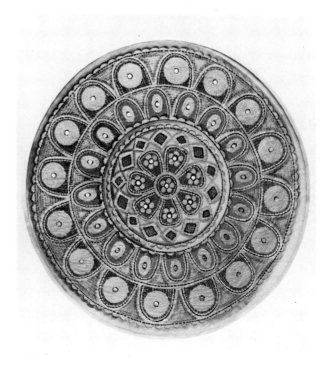

93

9-11. Marked color sketch of the same motif. Gold thread and several shades of the ground fabric are used in the embroidery.

9-10. An evening gown in the style of *shalvar* presented by Turkish mannequin Fatosh Altinkum. (From the archives of Istanbul Olgunlashma Enstitüsü; photographed by Teknika Laboratories.) *Shalvar* means baggy pants gathered around the ankles, as used in harems and in peasant folk costumes.

9-12. Drawing of the design on the evening gown. Details of this design, on the left, can be used as decorations elsewhere. The round design would make a lovely buckle. Any of the floral designs can be used individually.

9-13. A pants suit in the form of *shalvar* (see 9-10) pants and a sleeveless coat of satin, framed with fur. It is presented by Turkish mannequin Fatosh Altinkum. (From the archives of Istanbul Olgunlashma Enstitüsü; photographed by Teknika Laboratories.)

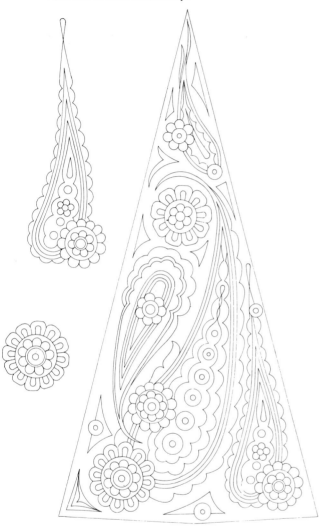

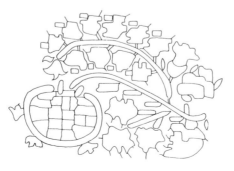

9-14. Drawing of a design that can be applied to a garment. White, green, and gold are used in *sira ishi*, *gözeme* and *sarma* stitches. The lines inside the oval design should be worked with *gözeme* stitch. This design is quite similar but not exactly the same as that used on the coat of the pants suit.

9-15. A dressy suit designed by one of Turkey's leading fashion designers, Zühal Yorgancioğlu. Presented by Turkish mannequin Safak Fishek, photographed by Mustafa Kapkin.

9-16. Drawing of the design on the sleeves of the suit, embroidered with *sarma* and *sira ishi*.

10 Embroidered Garments and Accessories

The photographs of the embroidered garments in this chapter indicate the endless variety of designs and placements on various parts of garments. They should serve as an inspiration for you to create your own fashions by embroidering the designs given in this book at appropriate places on your garments.

Embroidered accessories are also shown to give an idea of how traditional Turkish embroidery is applied to contemporary pocket books, cases for eyeglasses, and scarves.

10-1. A black-and-white evening gown designed by Zühal Yorgancioğlu. Presented by Turkish mannequin Sezin Topchuoğlu; photographed by Mustafa Kapkin.

10-2. An evening gown created by Zühal Yorgancioğlu. Presented by Turkish mannequin Hülya Korel; photographed by Mustafa Kapkin.

10-3. An evening gown embroidered in black. The embroideries are Nuriye Gürkök Sabuncuoğlu's creations. Presented by Turkish mannequin Meltem Karapazar. (From the archives of Istanbul Olgunlashma Enstitüsü; photographed by Teknika Laboratories.)

10-4. A pants suit presented by Turkish mannequin Füsun Ayanoğlu. Nuriye Gürkök Sabuncuoğlu designed the embroideries. (From the archives of Istanbul Olgunlashma Enstitüsü; photographed by Teknika Laboratories.)

10-5. A dress with embroideries on the sleeves.

10-6 and 10-7. Two dressy pocket books. On sale at Butik Lion in the Istanbul Hilton.

10-8 and 10-9. Two cases for eyeglasses. On sale at Butik Lion in the Istanbul Hilton.

10-10. An embroidered scarf. On sale at Butik Lion in the Istanbul Hilton.

Sources of Supply

Needle easels:
Pandora Manufacturing, c/o Joan Toggitt, Ltd. (wholesaler), 1170 Broadway, New York, N.Y. 10001 (handframes, table frames, floor frames).

Macy's Needlework Department, Herald Square, New York, N.Y. (standing frames).

Sperry and Son, 605 Main Street, Hyannis, Mass. 02601 (mail order for custom-made standing needlework frames).

Tracing paper, stamping powder and paste, perforating wheels:
New York Paper Company, 347 West 36th Street, New York, N.Y. (Strathmore perforating bond #106, stamping powder, stamping paste).

Sam Flax, 25 East 28th Street, New York, N.Y. (tracing paper in various thicknesses, charcoal, whiting, pounce wheels, also called perforating or tracing wheels).

Dritz-Scovill (wholesaler), Needle-pointed Tracing Wheel, Sewing Notions Division, Scovill Manufacturing Company, (wholesaler) Spartanburg, S.C. 29301.

French Sewing Basket, 1374 1st Ave. New York, N.Y.

Tinsel Trading, see below.

thin, flat metallic thread (tinsel or plate)
Progress Metallic Embroidery Thread (no. 920) c/o Macy's Needlework Department, Herald Square, New York, N.Y.

Tinsel Trading 47 West 38th Street, New York, N.Y. (large and small spools of flat and round metal threads in a great variety of shades, textures, and spins; write for brochure on Lamé Color Rack).

Silk or Rayon Thread:
Zwicky silk thread (in a wide range of colors) imported from Switzerland by Boutique Margot, 26 West 54th Street, New York, N.Y. 10019.

Springer-Marlitt Bella Donna rayon thread, imported by Joan Toggitt, Ltd. (wholesaler), 1170 Broadway, New York, N.Y. 10001.

Needles:
Any sharp needle with a large eye will be appropriate; these are often called crewel needles and can be bought in most needlework departments.

Silver and gold thread:
Thin, round thread (filé or lamé)
Dritz Metallic Thread (no. 616), Sewing Notions Division, Scovill Manufacturing Company (wholesaler), Spartanburg, S.C. 29301.

D.M.C. Corporation (wholesaler), 107 Trumbull Street, Elizabeth, N.J. 07206.

Index